THE POWER OF LOVE

"We're here on earth to learn to let go of fear and to learn to express unconditional love. As part of the process we learn that life is what we make it. And hopefully we learn the most important lesson of all. *Life is to be enjoyed!*"

—DICK SUTPHEN

Psychic researcher, past-life therapist and seminar trainer Dick Sutphen is the author of over 300 self-help tapes and 10 metaphysical books, including the best-selling *Past Lives, Future Loves; You Were Born Again to Be Together* and *Unseen Influences* (available from Pocket Books). Dick Sutphen has appeared on many major television shows, and performed the first nationally broadcast past-life regression on Tom Snyder's NBC "Tomorrow Show." Since 1977, 75,000 people have attended his world-famous seminars throughout the United States. Dick and his wife, Tara, live in Malibu, California.

Books by Dick Sutphen

Past Lives, Future Loves
Predestined Love
Unseen Influences
You Were Born Again to Be Together

Published by POCKET BOOKS

Most Pocket Books are available at special quantity discounts for bulk purchases for sales promotions, premiums or fund raising. Special books or book excerpts can also be created to fit specific needs.

For details write the office of the Vice President of Special Markets, Pocket Books, 1230 Avenue of the Americas, New York, New York 10020.

DICK SUTPHEN

PRE-DESTINED LOVE

POCKET BOOKS

New York London Toronto Sydney Tokyo

Another *Original* publication of POCKET BOOKS

POCKET BOOKS, a division of Simon & Schuster, Inc.
1230 Avenue of the Americas, New York, N.Y. 10020

Copyright © 1988 by Dick Sutphen
Cover photo copyright © 1988 Paccione Photography Inc.

ISBN: 0-671-64613-3

First Pocket Books printing April 1988

10 9 8 7 6 5 4 3 2 1

POCKET and colophon are trademarks of
Simon & Schuster, Inc.

Printed in the U.S.A.

With special thanks to
Jess Stearn,
who introduced me to my
wife and soulmate,
Tara,
who encouraged me to
write another book
about the power
of love

Many thanks to Sharon Boyd and Sherry Rueger for their help on this book.

The chapter titled "Cause and Its Effect on Marcie McGyver" was originally published in *Master of Life*, a Sutphen Corporation magalog sent to book/tape buyers.

Contents

CONTENTS

CHAPTER

1

You Were Born Again to Be Together

"If you were born again to be together, why are you now divorced and remarried to someone else?" the radio talk-show host asked. His voice was courteous but patronizing.

"I can't answer that with a simple statement," I replied.

"Why not? You've written books about reincarnation and how people are destined to be together. Doesn't your own divorce disprove your theory?" He sat back in his chair, smiling slyly, and took a long drag on his cigarette.

A microphone sat on the desk in front of me—an open line to over a hundred thousand Los Angeles listeners. "To be destined to be together doesn't necessarily mean you are destined to be together for an entire lifetime. Relationships can also be destined to end. A couple can be drawn together for . . ."

"Oh, come on, Richard," he interrupted. "Isn't all this just a slick rationale to justify your attractions and failures?"

How do you respond to someone who wants simplistic answers to complex questions? My talk-show host makes his living playing devil's advocate to authors, politicians, psychics, or whoever else the station programmer schedules to be interviewed. I've been asked the same questions in interviews all over the country by hosts who think of reincarnation as "cosmic foo-foo" to bolster their ratings.

"Let me briefly explain about soulmates, and hear me out if you will," I said. My voice was insistent. "A soulmate relationship is simply a love that is destined to be, and it always fits into three basic categories.

"*Karmic Companions* are two people destined to form a union to confront unlearned lessons from past lives. In other words, conflict is destined as a self-test to see if the principals have learned to let go of fear and respond with unconditional love. When I say unconditional love I don't mean romantic love—I'm talking about acceptance of others without expectations, judgment or blame.

"These relationships can be karmically structured in one of three ways: Locked-in—the players must remain together to resolve their conflicts; Open-ended—the outcome of the relationship depends upon the growth of the partners. If love matures, they will remain together. But if stagnation destroys the potential for spiritual growth, a parting is assured; and Destined-to-end—for the growth opportunity the parting provides. Can the two people let go with love . . . without excessive hostility, anger, and desire for revenge? If not, another mating in a future life is assured."

"What if one partner learns his lessons in this life and the other does not?" asked my host. His eyes shifted from his notes to me.

"The one who learned will not need to come back

12

with the other soul again. The soul still in need of awareness will be paired in the future with another whose karmic configuration matches his own. Whatever the reasons for the ending, for those who are willing to risk, a new 'destined' relationship probably awaits. Everything that has ever happened in the lives of both people prior to the initial meeting has prepared them for each other. They will have similar karmic needs, and the new relationship will allow them to continue to learn what they need to learn."

"Okay, Richard, what is the second kind of soulmate?"

"*Dharmic Bond Soulmates* share a goal. Everything I said about Karmic Companions also applies here, but the couple comes together, combining their energy to accomplish a joint task. At the point the shared goal is launched, established, or complete, the couple will have fulfilled their duty to themselves and each other. From then on their future together depends upon how they have karmically structured the relationship. It can be locked-in, open-ended or destined-to-end."

"What is dharma?" asked my talk-show host, as he poured two cups of black coffee, passing one over to me. For a moment I thought I might even have him interested.

"Dharma is your duty to yourself and society. Karma conditions you through all your experiences to create the character required to fulfill your dharma." He looked at me as if I were speaking Chinese, but didn't interrupt, so I continued with my explanation of the third kind of soulmate relationship.

"*Counterpart Soulmates* experience a loving, supportive relationship in which the partners share their lives with each other without conflict. That doesn't mean that they won't have problems, it is just that the problems will not be with each other. Most likely, they will have shared a long lineage of prerequisite lifetimes, and I feel that both people will have attained very close, or matching vibrational rates. In other words, they harmonize with each other, and the relationship is a karmic reward that will usually last for a lifetime . . . and maybe into future lifetimes, if they will it to be."

"Does predestined love always mean a soulmate relationship?" asked the host.

"Not in the context of being lovers," I replied. "Children, family members, and important friends are also predestined."

The remainder of the hour was filled with listener call-ins. Each caller wanted me to respond to his relationship situation. Every phone line was tied up with callers awaiting their turn. The show host had asked that I answer the questions as quickly as possible so more people could be answered rather than dealing in depth with just a few. This allowed me to make a philosophical point or two but certainly didn't serve the listeners. I left the station frustrated, as I had many times before on other programs in other cities. After doing over four hundred radio and TV interview shows, I know it's impossible to win them all.

"I'm going to write another book about this," I promised myself as I got into my car for the drive back to my home in Malibu. In the weeks that followed, I began to assemble my research on the subject of pre-destined love. In the ten years since I wrote *You Were Born Again to Be Together* and other metaphysical titles for Pocket Books, I've conducted metaphysical/self-help seminars in approximately twenty-four cities per year. Seventy-five thousand people have attended these gatherings, which run from one evening to seven days.

The participants come in search of themselves,

14

their earthly purpose, and a greater awareness of their human potential. At the end of each seminar, I ask the attendees to write to me about their experiences, any follow-up verification they obtain, and related experiences. The request generates an incredible amount of mail.

Some of the most interesting cases are followed up with phone calls in which I ask for additional information. In some situations, I arrange to work with the individuals, using metaphysical investigative techniques such as past-life regression, automatic writing, and psychometry.

Rather than merely reprint letters and explain the situation in typical nonfiction fashion, I have chosen to dramatize the case histories in this volume—based upon what I've been told and upon my follow-up interviews, investigations, and experiences.

This is a different approach to a New Age book, similar to a television docudrama. The technique results in rapid reading and easy assimilation of sometimes complicated metaphysical concepts. My goal is communication pointing to liberation *of* the self and *from* the self. Each case is based upon actual situations. Only a few of the names have been changed to protect the identity of the subjects.

Walk in peace, balance, and harmony,

Dick Sutphen
Malibu, California
June 1987

CHAPTER

2

Debra Wakefield's False Guilt Karma

Desperation drove Debra Wakefield to attend the 1979 reunion of her biological mother's family. At age thirty-one, it would be the first time she had seen her relatives in twenty-eight years. The gathering was to be held Sunday afternoon at Aunt Rosie Hart's, near Madras, Oregon. Eighteen aunts, uncles, cousins, and their families would be attending from all over the Pacific Northwest.

Debra turned left off Highway 97 at the white steepled church, onto a deeply rutted dirt road that wound past small family farms. The note containing the hastily written instructions bounced in her lap as she fought to keep the Nova out of the ruts. Right turn at Miller Road. One farmhouse looked like the next, and all in need of paint and repairs. The windows were tall and thin, reminiscent of another era. Each faded front-age was topped by a small attic window which she noticed uneasily.

Rosie's home was a duplicate of all the others she had passed since leaving the highway. Children were playing in the yard. Cars filled the drive, overflowing into a neat line running along the edge of the road. Debra emerged from her car, straightened the formal blue suit she had picked for the occasion, and gathered her composure around her like a fragile shell.

No one knew her until she explained who she was. Then they spoke warm, friendly words, while their faces wore masks of uneasy compassion. They carefully pretended not to look at her hands. She noticed the whispering when her back was turned, but she didn't care. The small talk was painful but necessary. There was enough food on the buffet to feed an army. Finally, she was alone with Rosie.

"Aunt Rosie, what can you tell me about my mother's death?" Debra asked. She spoke with a quiet but desperate firmness.

"There isn't much to tell, child," Rosie said. Her eyebrows drew together in an agonized expression. "You were about one and a half when she went into the hospital. She told me at the time she had no intention of ever coming out—she hated your father so much she didn't want to live any more. The medical reports showed nothing physically wrong, but she complained so much of abdominal pains they performed exploratory surgery. She died of complications from the surgery because it was the only way she could die."

Debra's face was grim. She stared at the worn patterns in the living room rug.

"Do you remember your father at all?" Rosie asked, her voice betraying a critical tone.

Debra shook her head. "Not really, only flashes in therapy."

"Therapy?"

"I seem to have blocked all memories of my early childhood, Aunt Rosie." Debra shrugged her shoulders. She was kneading one hand with the other. "All my life I've felt bone cold inside, and I've ached right here." She drew her hands tightly against her stomach. "I joined a personal growth gestalt class a few months ago and terrible things started surfacing in the group processes. I don't know if they're real or imagined and they're driving me crazy. I decided to make contact with my real family again."

"What terrible things?" Rosie asked, tension noticeable in her voice.

"I relived a situation . . . I must have been about two years old and I was sitting in the living room holding my kitten. I guess my father called me, but I didn't hear him. In a rage, he came up behind me, grabbed the kitten, pulled out his knife, and cut its head off. He threw the body in my lap. The head was laying on the floor, its eyes staring up at me. I started to scream and scream . . . there was blood everywhere. Then he wiped the bloody knife across my face, yelling, 'You loved the kitten more than you love me. It's your fault it's dead. And it's your fault your mother is dead.'" Debra was shaking and the words seemed to wedge in her throat.

"Oh, my child. Oh, my God." Rosie held both hands to her mouth. She took the few steps to the couch and sat down.

Debra stood motionless in the middle of the room looking down at her aunt. In the background she could hear the drone of conversation from the front porch. A cousin walked through the living room on her way to the kitchen.

"It's true, Debra. Your brother Tommy talked about it at the trial. You must realize, to your mother's side of the family, your father was a monster."

"Then why didn't they put him away?" She spat out the words contemptuously.

Rosie hesitated, nodding slowly. "Do you remember what happened, just before the state took you away from him?"

"I've heard the story, but you tell me what you know." She was kneading her hands once more.

"Your father locked you and Tommy in the attic. After 24 hours without water, you became very ill. Tommy broke out to run for help. But Mr. Kloss—as your father demanded to be called—caught him. He grabbed a rope, tied it around Tommy's neck, and hung him from the overhang of the house. Neighbors saw what was happening and came running to Tommy's rescue. They were just in time—a few more minutes and your brother would surely have died. They called the police. Tommy was taken to the hospital, and you and your sister were taken to foster homes."

"Which were no better," Debra snapped.

"Child, after your mother died, Mr. Kloss cut off all contact with our side of the family. We didn't know about any of this until the trial, years later. By then the Wakefield family was legally fighting to adopt you. We just didn't know."

On the drive back to Portland, the broken yellow line down the center of the highway flashed hypnotically in Debra's peripheral vision. Flick, flick, flick. She shook her head to clear it, attempting to fit the pieces of new knowledge into the puzzle of her life. Flick, flick, flick—she was back in the personal growth gestalt class, lying on the floor with her eyes closed, crying.

"Go to your level, go where it hurts," said the soft voice of her instructor.

"Can't! Can't! Can't!" screamed the two-year-old in her mind.

"Yes, you can, Debra. Bring in someone you can trust."

"There's no one to trust." Debra's voice hardened.

"No one single person you know?"

"No."

"Can you trust God?"

"No . . . NO, NO, NO!"

"What about Jesus? Can you trust Jesus?"

She didn't answer.

"Debra, can't you trust Jesus?"

"Yes . . . I think so."

"Then will you let Jesus help you examine your childhood?"

"Yes."

"All right, go where it hurts."

"Hands hurt . . . hands hurt." She began sobbing in wretched, tormented sobs.

"What is happening, Debra? Speak up and tell me what is happening."

"She . . . she put my hands in washer." The bloodcurdling cry erupting from the depths of Debra's throat awakened the four other students in the class. They sat up, their anxiety expressed by their protective body language.

In a calm voice, the instructor asked, "You mean someone put your hands in the wringer of a washing machine?"

"Ah, huh . . . she, she . . . oh-h-h-h-h." The childish voice of consciously forgotten anguish did not seem to belong to the beautiful adult woman writhing on the floor.

"Who did this?"

"She, she . . . oh-h-h-h."

Further attempts to obtain information were unsuccessful. Debra's only response was sobs and an anguished, "Hands hurt . . . hands hurt."

"Okay, breathe in the relaxation once again, Debra. You will awaken calm and relaxed, remembering everything you've just experienced on the count of five.

20

"Can you talk about it?" the instructor asked after providing a box of tissues and a glass of water. The other students, forming a semicircle on the floor, leaned closer to catch every word. The only sound in the room was Debra's sniffled breathing.

"Oh, God," she said weakly, pausing to drink and rub her swollen eyes. "I've been told about what happened, but until now I had no memory of it." Her voice was choked and raw, and the words seemed strange on her tongue. "After I was taken away from my father, I was placed in foster homes. At the age of two and a half, someone—presumably my foster mother—ran my hands through the wringer of an old-fashioned washing machine and left me hanging by my bleeding hands over the edge of the washer." Debra limply lifted her hands as if a puppeteer had raised two strings. The terrible scars ran halfway up her forearms—multicolored, mangled flesh had subsequently healed into abstract patterns of pain.

The other students stared, then looked away. The instructor, seated on the floor beside Debra, had knotted her right hand into a fist which she pressed against her own mouth as if to quell the feelings arising within.

Debra took a slow, audible breath. Her eyes were cold and passionless as she continued. "Another foster child, a five-year-old boy, heard my moans and helped me get down. He wrapped the wounds in dirty handkerchiefs. The foster parents were gone. We had been abandoned in the ramshackle house."

"What happened?" asked a woman in her mid-twenties, clasping her knees tightly to her chest.

Debra looked down at her hands. She unconsciously kneaded one with the other and spoke almost mechanically now. "I was told that for the first time in twenty years, a state social worker drove home a different way. Passing our house, she saw what appeared to be a child in distress and stopped to check. I was walking back and forth on the front steps saying, 'hands hurt, hands hurt.' I held them up to the woman. Gangrene was setting in. She rushed me to the hospital."

The tears slowly formed in the corner of Debra's eyes, and listlessly trailed down her cheeks. As the instructor put her arm around Debra, she collapsed, sobs racking her body.

"It's all right, Debra. You're processing through the pain and it's going to get better now."

"Are you sure?"

"The pain has to come out. I want you to finish the story." The instructor spoke in a soft, reassuring tone, with rhythmic pacing. "You have the strength. You have the strength. You have the strength." Debra lay limply in her instructor's arms until the sobbing abated. As she sat up, her eyes met those of the other students, who smiled encouragingly.

"Can you finish the story, Debra?"

She nodded affirmatively. "The doctors at the hospital wanted to amputate my arms. But one surgeon had recently studied new medical procedures. He'd even taken home a severed arm to study how to save others in the future. He saved my arms.

"Donalie Wakefield was at the Salem hospital that night awaiting her husband, a doctor on staff. When I was released she took me home to her family of three daughters. I'm told she held and rocked me for hours at a time, whispering, "No one will ever hurt you again."

"So the Wakefields adopted you?"

"No, not right away. The laws were very difficult at the time—in those days, biological parents had all the rights, no matter what they did to their children. A few years later my father, Mr. Kloss, wanted me back. At that time the Wakefields could fight him in court. My new mom said our attorney was light-years ahead of his time and he won a judgment that set new precedents for the rights of abused children in the state of Oregon. Mr. Kloss' attorney ended up being disbarred for the way he conducted himself. The court ordered my father never to contact me again. He never did."

"Where is he today?" asked one of the students.

"I've heard he is running a business in southern California. It's all I want to know."

The headlights of the oncoming vehicle flashed high and low, high and low, jolting Debra back into her present reality. She snapped her lights to low beam and straightened her cramped, stiff body in the seat. The white letters on the roadsign flashed past on the right: PORTLAND 25.

"Portland is a boring city," Robert had said. Was that six years ago? No, seven. "You've got a boring job in a boring city and you're the most screwed-up woman I've ever seen, but I love you anyway." He was a classmate in her graduating class at the University of Hawaii, and he had followed her from the Islands to Portland.

"Why do you think I attended so many colleges?" she asked him.

"I don't know."

"I changed colleges every time a man proposed to me. It was easiest to respond by quietly disappearing."

"As the prettiest girl on campus, you had to expect us men to fall in love with you," Robert laughed.

They were in a restaurant when Robert formally proposed marriage, placing an open jeweler's box containing a ring on the table before her. Debra set her drink down. She looked at the diamond reflecting the dancing candlelight as she grasped the table edge with both hands. Her mouth was tight and grim. Unspoken pain reflected in her cool blue eyes, now ablaze with emotion. Her knuckles were white and her body trembled.

"Debra, I love you," he said, gently placing his hand upon her shoulder. "Don't you understand, I really lo . . ."

"NO-O-O-O-O!" Her voice was a hysterical growl. "NO-O-O-O-O!" Raw, primitive emotion exploded, shattering the romantic atmosphere of the restaurant. The other patrons turned to see her push the table forward with all her strength. It tipped. Glass shattered. "NO-O-O-O-O!" She was standing now, her head to one side, shaking convulsively, floundering blindly in her agony.

"Has it really been seven years since that night?" Debra thought as the lights of Portland appeared on the horizon. "Poor Robert. I didn't understand it any better than he did . . . until today. Until Aunt Rosie showed me the picture of Mr. Kloss. Amazing. He looked almost exactly like Robert."

1980–1981: While offering little of therapeutic value, the gestalt class convinced Debra that she needed professional help. A special Dale Carnegie course for adults abused in childhood proved to be of value in dealing with the intense anger still locked inside. Her first real therapy was with a counselor at the Unity Guidance Center. After three months, she started to come out of the oppressive mental turmoil, but was unable to resolve the desolate coldness and painful feeling of impending catastrophe in the pit of her stomach.

1982: "Something has to happen, God," Debra said aloud during meditation. "It can't go on like this. Please. Something has to happen."

In the following day's mail was a magazine containing an advertisement for a *Know Thy Higher Self— Sutphen Seminar* to be held in Maui, Hawaii, April 19–

25. Goose bumps ran up and down Debra's arms as she read the copy:

HAWAII 7 DAY GETAWAY, Including an ALL YOU ARE CAPABLE OF BEING Seminar.

A small group of people will spend a week renewing body, mind and spirit on the beautiful beach of Kaanapali in Maui, Hawaii. Past-life therapist Dick Sutphen will direct the 20-hour seminar. Explore the past-life and present-life cause of conflicts in your life, and examine your potential to become all you are capable of being. Participants will learn several metaphysical techniques for self-exploration which they will be able to use for the rest of their lives.

Let Kaanapali Beach become a point of departure for your spirit. To walk on a morning along the beach, in the long shadows of the West Maui Mountains, is to be conscious of the process of renewal and reawakening that is at work within the soul.

"I got goose bumps when I read the ad," Debra explained to her sister, Joy. "To me, goose bumps are always an affirmation of truth. If you went, too, it would cut expenses to the point where I might be able to afford it."

"I wish I could, Debra, but there's no way. And I really doubt you could get off work for a week," Joy replied reluctantly.

That night Debra carried her problem into meditation. "Okay, God, if this is what you'd like me to do, then you're going to have to do it, because I know they won't let me off work and even if they did, I can't afford it."

Before the week was out Joy called. "Debra, do you still want to go to Hawaii? I can get off, and I've even come up with some extra money."

"I don't believe it," Debra stammered. "This morning my boss told me I could have the time off if I still wanted it."

Maui, Hawaii: In the second session of the *All You Are Capable of Being* seminar, the participants were taught automatic writing. "As I'm sure every one in this room is aware, automatic writing is a channeling technique in which you allow another entity or your own Higher Self to express through your hands. The secret to successful automatic writing is self-trust. You must mentally let go enough to allow awareness to be channeled through your hand. I'll be inducing an altered state of consciousness to make this easier. In the first exercise I want you to allow a character of wisdom to express something that would be of value for you to know about at this time."

"What if an earthbound, or low-level entity comes through?" asked one of the participants.

"At the beginning of the exercise I'll be directing an intense, white God light protection. Since we cannot be influenced by unseen entities with vibrational rates lower than our own, most metaphysical people certainly don't 'need' protection. But if your aura has been weakened by drug-taking, excessive alcohol, illness, extreme negativity, hatefulness, or depression, your vibrational rate can be temporarily reduced. So even if your natural protection is down, I bring it back up while I am working with you to assure that you receive only accurate perceptions. An earthbound entity can influence you as easily while you are fully conscious as when you are in an altered state."

"Can we ask questions of whomever is writing through our hands?" asked another participant.

"Yes. I wouldn't interrupt the flow of writing, but if it seems appropriate, you can take control of your pen and write out the question. Or some people prefer to mentally ask and then await the writing to begin again. Unless there are further questions, this is how we'll proceed. I want you to sit, be as relaxed as possible, and put both feet flat on the floor. Hold your pen loosely in your writing hand and your pad in the other. I'll hypnotize you, using the technique you're already familiar with. After invoking the protection, I'll direct you across a symbolic bridge into your Higher Self. At this point, after giving you very strong suggestions that you have the power and ability to successfully use automatic writing as a channel for higher awareness, I will instruct you to open your eyes and allow the writing to begin to come through. Don't open your eyes wide. Attempt to maintain that soft-focus level. Stare blankly at the paper and relax your mind. The lighting in the room will be very low, and special music will be playing softly. The music is combined with a hypnagogic, theta-level sound vibration that will assist you to remain at the proper level to successfully complete the exercise."

Debra easily followed the body relaxation, and mentally participated in the protective ritual: "Draw down a beam of shimmering, iridescent, bright white God light and feel it enter the crown chakra of spirituality on the top of your head. This is the Universal light of life energy and you create a channel for the light with the unlimited power of your mind. Feel the light begin to flow through your body and mind, and imagine it concentrating around your heart area. And now perceive the light emerging from your heart area to surround your body and mind with a protective aura of bright white God light. And you are totally protected. Only your own guides and Masters, or highly evolved and loving entities who mean you well, will be able to influence you in any way. We ask it, we beseech it, we mark it . . . and so it is."

Debra could feel her body becoming lighter and lighter as she floated along with the suggestions to ascend into Higher Self. "Ascending, transcending, crossing over . . ." She felt she was floating as the final instructions filled her mind. "On the count of three, a very wise soul will channel through your hand. One, two, three."

Debra's hand twitched, then stopped. She held the soft-pointed pen loosely and looked at the paper through distanced, dull eyes. She was there in the room with the others but she wasn't. The music sounded like celestial harmonies—angels humming in her ear as she walked an endless white sand beach.

Hello my Child, her hand moved forming words very different from her own feminine script. *We are pleased that you have returned. We have always guided you along the way.* The pen stopped. She waited. Nothing. HOW CAN I BE SURE THIS IS REAL? she wrote. *How can you be sure that it is not?* her hand responded. *You seek our assistance, but it must come from within you. You want to experience the fullness and richness of life.* WHO IS SPEAKING TO ME? *My name is Samuel.* WHY ISN'T MY LIFE GOING ANYWHERE? *It is—you just don't recognize the path. Remember the story about the little boy who wants to be a doctor? He must first grow up and do many things to prepare himself for that role. You too are preparing for a role, but it is still best that you don't know. You must discover your own path or it will not be valid for you. You've worked very hard and we are proud of the work you are doing.* THIS IS STUPID! *See—you do not accept. Remember how hard you have been working on acceptance? You have made great strides, but you still have a way to go. We are here on the other side, guiding you along each step of the way.*

Although you may not consciously realize it, you have been listening well. Awareness is forthcoming, our child. YOU SAID 'MY CHILD' AT THE BEGINNING. *There are many of us with you.* BUT YOU'RE THE ONE WHO HAS TALKED TO ME. *You will meet more of us soon.* YOU HAVEN'T GIVEN ME ANY ANSWERS. *Yes we have, if you choose to find them. The exercise is about over. We love you.*

Upon awakening, Debra reread the automatic writing and shook her head. She listened quietly as some of the participants shared what they received. "I don't know if I can accept it," she said to Joy over lunch. The restaurant was outside, overlooking the beach. Gently blowing palm trees cast lazy shadows across the table. Beyond the sunbathers, sleek bodies glistening with suntan oil, was the hotel sailboat concession. Debra smiled at the novice sailors attempting unsuccessfully to launch a Sunfish sailboat into the surf.

"Do you think you made it up?" Joy asked.

"I don't know, Joy. If I did, it seems to me I could have made up something a bit more interesting. My hand certainly seemed to have a mind of its own. But it almost seems too easy."

"Debra, you've never been one to accept easy answers."

Debra's face spread into a wide grin. "Thanks a lot."

"This first session after lunch is going to be an automatic writing dialogue with our body. That ought to be interesting," Joy said, squeezing a roll of excess weight around her middle.

"I'm going to ask why I'm having a herpes flare-up this week." Debra's voice was a whisper, to avoid being overheard by the people at surrounding tables.

29

"Better yet, ask why you caught it in the first place. As little as you've had to do with men, it's almost ironic," Joy whispered back.

"It's men in general, Joy. I have wonderful karma with men. Or haven't you noticed?" There was ice in her husky whisper.

In the afternoon automatic writing exercise, on the count of three, Debra's hand moved quickly. *No your herpes outbreak is not from the sun or the class. We are . . .* WHO IS WE? *Why, your cells, of course. We are having to make some chemical changes in your body due to your changing beliefs. As you slowly let go of your anger relating from your childhood, we must begin functioning on a new basis. Then you will feel confident, strong and healthy. We are pleased that you treat us fairly well. We're sorry to have made you uncomfortable, but the herpes will be gone in two days. And thank you for giving us permission to teach you what serves us and you. May we suggest more vitamin C. Also take L-Lysine and the other medicine you are already using. Stop eating so much oil. We know you are concerned about your fingernails. Take more calcium, zinc, and magnesium three times a day. And bless them. Your hands are beautiful. They have done no wrong that you should continue to punish them and think them evil. Your hands are kind and loving and gentle. They will assist you to accomplish your dreams if you will love them.* WHY SO MUCH ON MY HANDS? WHAT ABOUT MY LEGS? *Your legs are hardest to change because you hang onto your belief about their present shape so strongly.*

The final automatic writing session of the afternoon was to focus upon each participant's earthly purpose. The trance level seemed deeper to Debra as she attempted to hold on to the soft edge of reality, ascending into Higher Self. Again, her pen began writing immediately upon the count of three.

You don't really want to know your purpose because you are afraid of your feelings. The purpose of everyone on earth is to resolve fear and express unjudgmental love. But you think if you don't know what your fears are, they will go away. This is not true. Until you understand your fears, you will continue to punish yourself. Your fears are all based upon guilt you experience from your past. It is time to love yourself, to forgive yourself, and to stop punishing yourself for something you didn't do. WHAT DO YOU MEAN, 'PUNISH MYSELF'? *You and you alone are responsible for your experiences. Your beliefs generate your thoughts and emotions which form your reality.* BUT I'VE DONE EVERYTHING I CAN THINK OF TO HELP MYSELF. WHAT MORE CAN I DO? *You respond to yourself like a mean, shriveled-up old lady. You have no rights. You don't deserve any desires. You are evil and bad and should be punished. This is not you, but since you believe it to be, it is. You cannot accept that others could care for you. Even when you try very hard to accept or believe the loving words and gestures, the old lady in you will have none of it. She will always find a way to create negativity in the relationship. On another level of mind you knew James had herpes. The only reason you made love to him was to contract the disease and further punish yourself.* I DON'T UNDERSTAND ANY OF THIS. WHAT CAN I DO? *You can give her back her hands! She loved and expressed love through her hands. You were just using Raimondo and she really loved him. But you were so jealous that you wouldn't let another woman have him. You have carried her hate with you for lifetimes. Give her back her hands!* WHAT ARE YOU

31

TALKING ABOUT? *The exercise is over. He awakens you now. We love you, our child.*

The last half hour of the afternoon was spent having the participants read their automatic writing. I responded with encouragement or attempted to provide karmic interpretations of the information from the other side. Debra raised her hand to share and I pointed to her. She was an attractive woman of thirty-three, with cinnamon-colored hair. I wondered why she was dressed so formally in Hawaii.

"This is really weird," she began. After reading the automatic writing, she said, "What does it mean, give her back her hands? Where did that come from? I just can't accept this as anything but babbling."

Admitting I didn't have her answers, I suggested she volunteer to be the subject of the first individual regression the following afternoon. "I want to conduct some individual in-depth past-life regression sessions. It sounds like the message may relate back to a previous incarnation, Debra." She agreed, and I told her to bring her tape recorder to record the session.

A Hawaiian dinner show was the evening's entertainment, and Debra and her sister sat far off to the side of the proceedings. In an effort to be a good host, I stopped by their table to ask how they were doing. Everyone else in the room was dressed for the hot night but Debra was wearing a sports coat over a high-necked blouse. As she raised her drink to her lips, I noticed the terrible scars on her hands and wrists. "Is this your first visit to Hawaii?" I asked.

"Oh no, I went to school here," Debra replied. "Your seminar was just a great excuse to come back for a visit." She paused. "Richard, do you really think my automatic writing could be real?" There was a hopeful glint in her eye.

"I don't think all automatic writing is pure," I said carefully.

"Pure?"

"When someone channels, verbally or through automatic writing, there is often a scrambling of their own awareness and that of the source. Rather than concerning yourself about the validity of the contact, I would judge the accuracy by the advice itself . . . by the results."

"But you think the source is another entity . . . someone in spirit?" There was now an eagerness in her voice.

"You mean, do I think it's possible? I don't think it. I know it, based upon my own experience and the experiences of thousands of seminar participants. You can be in contact with your own Higher Self, the eternal energy of a discarnate entity, or your own guides and Masters. Automatic writing is my favorite technique to convert the skeptical. You saw Johnson in the session this afternoon. The only reason he's with us is to humor Patty. He's so in love that he was willing to escort her to a 'nutcake seminar,' to quote him. But after the last session, his belief system is in tatters. He was so successful at automatic writing, he has to fit the experience into his old ideas about existence. Naturally, the pieces aren't going to fit together. So he'll either have to deny his experience or change his ideas about the meaning of life."

"He won't deny his experience," Joy said flatly.

"Of course not," I agreed. "So another New Ager is added to the fold."

"Richard, in the first exercise, my wisdom character was named Samuel. He said he and a group help and guide me in my life. I didn't think you had more than one spirit guide," Debra said questioningly.

"You have only one primary guide, but you can

have others who back him up. My guide is an Indian woman named Neeta, but in my meditations I have the sense of an entire tribe of people offering supportive energy and protection."

"Ruth Montgomery uses automatic writing to create her books," Joy inserted. "Are Lilly and the group of twelve or so all her guides?"

"That's how I understand it," I said. "And my son Travis is also somehow related to that group energy. Ruth was receiving automatic writing about him before he was born."

"Has Neeta been with you since you were born?" Debra asked. She leaned forward in her chair, awaiting an answer.

"Yes. And she'll remain with me throughout my life. In meditation I asked her what she did to guide me and she explained that her efforts primarily consisted of providing intuitive feelings about my life directions. Maybe she's the force behind my concerns. Love is the power behind the guidance and she told me that we also often work together on the other side, when my physical body is asleep."

Debra and Joy were obviously interested so I continued. "Now, when I go into deep hypnosis and purposely travel to a subjective 'center' in my mind, Neeta is always there waiting for me. I see her with my inner eyes and hear her with my inner ears. She offers warnings, guidance, or encouragement. The communication takes place through thought language. Some metaphysicians call your primary guide a 'lifetime' guide. Others, usually those leaning toward Christian beliefs, perceive their unseen companion as a 'guardian angel.'"

The following afternoon Debra relaxed on a recliner in the hotel meeting room. A lapel microphone was pinned to her blouse to amplify her voice. I took a chair beside her and the lights in the room were dimmed. "All right, Debra, we want to investigate the things we talked about yesterday. We want to know the meaning of the phrase, 'give her back her hands.' But I'm also interested in exploring a primary problem in your life. Take a moment to think about a problem you'd like to explore."

"More than anything else, I'd like to understand my inability to have a relationship," she said softly. "I've never had a relationship last more than a couple of months."

I induced deep hypnosis and directed Debra into her Higher Self. "In the memory banks of your subconscious mind is a memory of everything you have ever experienced in this life or any of your previous lifetimes. Every thought, every spoken word, every action is recorded in the memory banks of your mind and we are now going to work together to draw forgotten understanding down into your conscious awareness. I want you to go back to the cause of the phrase, 'give her back her hands.' I'm going to count backward from five to one, and on the count of one, vivid impressions will come into your mind. Impressions that will help you understand your current life. Five, four, three, two, one. Allow the impressions to form. Speak up and tell me what you see and what you are doing."

"We're all laughing . . . my friends and I. We're around the pool." Debra's voice was light. The corners of her mouth formed a slight smile.

"Are you male or female?"

"Female. I am with seven of my girlfriends."

"How old are you?"

"Twenty-eight."

"What is the occasion of the party?"

"It isn't a party. We're getting ready to go to the festival."

"Where do you live?"

"Rome."

"All right, let's move forward in time until something very important happens. On the count of three you'll be there. One, two, three."

"IT WAS RAIMONDO WHO CUT OFF NEPHRI'S HANDS! Oh-o-o-o-o."

"Why?"

"He wanted me. He warned me if I didn't respond to him, something terrible would happen. Nephri loved him, but he cut off her hands to demonstrate what will happen to me unless I bend to his will."

"How could Raimondo do this without being punished himself?"

"He is very powerful. No one would punish him. I can heal with my hands. He knows how important my hands are to my work."

"All right, let's move forward in time to see how this works out. On the count of three, you will move forward far enough to be able to tell me the outcome. One, two, three."

"I left and went to a place where we were safe from Raimondo. Nephri came with me. She blames me for the loss of her hands. That's all she ever talks about. 'It's your fault I lost my hands, it's your fault I lost my hands.' Over and over and over. I stopped healing. I can't do it anymore." Debra stopped talking. Her jaw locked firmly and her eyes danced back and forth beneath closed eyelids. "SHE'S HERE RIGHT NOW. SHE'S STILL FOLLOWING ME AROUND. SHE ALWAYS FOLLOWS ME AROUND." Debra's voice was so loud over the microphone that the speakers distorted wildly. She spoke with an icy bitterness.

"IT'S NOT MY FAULT YOU LOST YOUR HANDS. I DIDN'T CUT THEM OFF, RAIMONDO DID. WHY CAN'T YOU UNDERSTAND THAT? Why? Why? Why?"

"Debra, I want you to take a very deep breath and relax. Allow the quietness of spirit to come in."

"She's right here, Richard. Right in this room, right now. She's laughing and she says she has been with me ever since Rome, waiting for me to give back her hands. Every time a man gets interested in me, she gets ugly. She thinks it's funny. She says I owe her. She says she is the cold—she's the ache in my gut that will never go away until I pay her back. But I don't know how to pay her back. I'm so afraid. I'm so afraid."

"You're safe and secure, Debra. Believe that. I want some of the other participants to come up and lay their hands upon Debra's arms and legs and feed her their energy. And I now call upon Samuel and Debra's guides to be with her and provide us with your energy from the other side of the veil. And to thee God, be the Kingdom, and the Power, and the Glory, unto the ages of ages. I seek Thy protection for Debra, from all things seen and unseen, all forces and all elements. In Thy Divine Name, we open to the light. We offer our bodies, our minds, and our spirits to the light. Let Thy Divine Will and mine be as one. As it is above, so it is below. I ask these things in Thy Name. I beseech it and I mark it. And so it is."

"NEPHRI DOESN'T LIKE THIS." Debra sputtered, her body arching against an unseen force.

"I'm sure she doesn't," I replied flatly. "Ask Nephri about the guilt. She has caused you to accept so much guilt you have created terrible circumstances in your life."

The room was a tomb of silence.

"Nephri," I now appealed directly to the earthbound spirit I knew was with us all. My voice was cold and commanding. A female participant next to me, sending energy into Debra's lower legs, was trembling uncontrollably. "Nephri, I want to communicate directly to you. You in turn can communicate your response to Debra who will relay it to me. Is this acceptable to you?"

"She says it is, but she is very upset," Debra said, her voice still agitated and fearful.

"Nephri, you're in pain. I know you are in pain. You're filled with hate, you're confused and I would go so far as to assume your hands still hurt. Is this so?" I asked.

"She says, 'Yes.' "

"Nephri, if you want to feel better, all you have to do is go to the light. I want you to look around and see where the light is coming from."

"She sees the light, but she says she isn't going anywhere without her hands."

"Nephri, Debra cannot give you back your hands. Only you can give yourself back your hands by letting go of the hatred and going to the light where you will attain help and understanding. Spirits have told you this before, but you've been unwilling to listen. Because of your blaming and hatred, you have suffered for two thousand years. It's time to resolve this. Debra was guilty of using a man you loved, but she did not cut off your hands. That was your karma. It was suffering you needed to experience. Now, it is time to go to the light."

There was a long silence while Debra's eyes moved rapidly beneath her eyelids, seeing the reality of the unseen. "She won't go to the light."

"Then I call upon Samuel to find someone that Nephri knew and trusted in her life in Rome. Someone who loved her very much." Goose bumps ran up and down my arms as I waited for Debra's next response.

"Nephri's mother is here. She is telling Nephri what you told her." Debra's facial muscles were relaxed for the first time. There was a flush in her cheeks. "She's going with her mother. She just turned and went with her mother. I don't believe it."

"You're free now, Debra. For the first time in your life, you're free. I don't mean to be corny, but this is literally the first day of the rest of your life. You can now go on to create any reality you want to live. Do you understand this?"

"Yes, oh yes."

Four days after the seminar, Debra Wakefield wrote me a four-page letter. The following is a condensation:

April 29, 1982—Dear Richard, Things have not stopped happening since the Maui experience! Just to mention a few: 1. I have not been "bone cold" since the regression. That is a first in my life; 2. Nephri visited me on the plane from Maui to Honolulu. I was sitting by myself, and just started to doze, when all of a sudden I felt very warm, yet goose-bumpy. Nephri said, "Thank you for taking care of me, and please forgive me. I've learned much from being with you, and I will send you many blessings." 3. Until now, I never knew how it felt to really like myself. I imagined what it must feel like, and I pretended—basically in Cinderella fashion—but I was forever "coping." I was also very negative. The very first thought in my mind was always a "worst-case" scenario. I had to work very hard to see things as good and positive. Sometimes I did better than others, but all in all, it's always been an uphill struggle. Much to my amazement, there is no struggle whatsoever now. I FEEL LIKE A DIFFERENT PERSON. The first thing everyone back home said was how healthy I look. Believe me, it's nothing compared to how I FEEL!!!!!

The next strange thing that happened is through automatic writing the first day I was back in Portland. Samuel and my guides said I would not be in my present job long (I don't particularly like accounting). Here are some of their words: *"We are glad you have contacted us and want to work with us. You no longer need to fear. We have prepared a career path you will like. For awhile it will be like a dream come true. We have much to do in a very short period of time, and we hope that you will keep in close contact with us. A suggestion for tomorrow is to bless EVERYTHING that happens to you. Say, 'I appreciate the good and all are blessed.' We also wish you would begin to use and trust your hands again. Touch people. Touch yourself and share your love."*

When I arrived at work today, I had a new job. I'm now assistant to the treasurer, setting up the cash management program for the company. When that is completed, I will go to school to learn about commercial real estate. I have a new office in the executive suite.

This is still all very strange to me, yet I feel so wonderful. I feel like I had to resolve the Nephri situation before I could begin to fulfill my destiny. And to the best of my knowledge, it's the first time in thirty-three years I have not been in some kind of emotional pain, sheer terror, or deathly cold. Thank you for being there and helping to free Nephri and me. I can truly say I AM HAPPY.

Thank you again, with all my heart, Debra.

January 1987: It had been five years since I talked to Debra Wakefield. I asked my staff to pull up her

Portland address on the computer. "There is no one by that name listed in Oregon," Mary told me. "The only Debra Wakefield in the computer lives in San Jose, California. She's been actively purchasing your self-help tapes for years."

I sent her a note: "Are you the Debra Wakefield from the Maui, Hawaii seminar? If so, I'd love to talk to you again." By return mail I received the reply and Debra's home and work phone numbers.

"Tell me about your life, Debra."

"It's wonderful, Richard. I just had to get things cleared up in Maui before I could meet my soulmate." There was a trace of laughter in her voice over the long distance phone line.

"I want to hear all about him," I said, settling back in my most comfortable chair with a large cup of after-dinner coffee.

"Well, his name is Bill Markham. I met him years ago, but he was married to someone else. But we always remained in contact with Christmas cards. After he was divorced he wrote, asking if he could come to Portland to visit. That was in October 1983. He just turned my world upside down. Within weeks he came to me with an engagement ring. He called it a 'statement' ring because it was so big and beautiful. He knew my background of fearing commitment and he wanted to show me how committed he was. And I must admit to being impressed. I thought, 'He must really love me to go this far.' After we were engaged I moved with him back to his home in San Jose."

"So it was a storybook romance, right from the start?" I asked.

"No, not exactly," she replied. "You see Bill is really overweight. I had never been able to tolerate overweight people. But I just loved him anyway. However, there was a period where I got cold feet. I even decided to write him a note and tell him I wanted out. So when I sat down to write, it didn't come out the way the words were forming in my head. My hand wrote, *My child, if you look at Bill through the eyes of love, you will be happier than your wildest heart's desire. But if you look at him through your physical eyes, you will always be disappointed.*

"And that's exactly how it worked out. Bill is the most beautiful soul I've ever known. I know I've waited my whole life, and lifetimes and lifetimes and lifetimes, to be with him."

CHAPTER

3

The Guidance of Rob Bradwick

The coffee cup flew past his head and shattered against the kitchen wall.

"I hate you!" she screamed, her body constricted and trembling as she reached for something else to throw.

"Ellen, please . . ." Rob pleaded without emotion as he knelt to pick up the pieces, more to avoid looking at his wife than out of any concern for the mess. "At the rate you're going through dishes, we'll be down to paper plates before the week's out," he stated flatly, tossing the pieces into a wastebasket.

"Then you'll have to buy some new ones. The cost of a night on the town with your favorite tramp would pay for a lot of dishes, wouldn't it?" she replied, a bitter edge of cynicism in her voice.

"Ellen!" He could feel the anger rising inside him and he didn't want to lose control. Not again.

"Is she really in love with you, Rob, or does she see you as a ticket for a matching Porsche?"

"I'm not in love with Susan and you know it," he snapped. "What good does it do to continually go over it? The next step is for you to tell me that I started it all by having an affair. Then I'll counter by bringing up your retaliatory romps with Arthur. We can throw names and accusations back and forth and it will end the way it always does—accomplishing nothing but more pain."

Ellen slowly lowered herself into a chair at the kitchen table, staring blankly at her husband. "I'm so tired of the pain," she said quietly.

"So am I."

"What are we going to do, Rob?"

His stomach twisted in anger. He looked at her, and for a brief moment, thought about how beautiful she was. He wished it could be good between them again. "I don't know what we're going to do, Ellen. The fact that we've gone on as long as we have must be some kind of masochistic endurance record."

"Maybe underneath it's hate that's holding us together," she replied without looking up. Her tone was defeated.

"Maybe."

Everything used to be so simple. They met in college, fell in love and were married the week after graduation. Their first child, Arlene, was born the following year. Jeffy followed two years later. Rob worked for a title company, eventually learning enough to start his own company. It was successful enough to enable them to move into a larger home in the most desirable suburb of Seattle.

Ellen had studied journalism in college. After graduation, she went on to a feature-writing position with the *Seattle Post*. When the children arrived, she made an easy transition to being a full-time wife and mother who free-lanced an occasional article for the paper. "Erma Bombeck rip-offs," she called her stories about the joys and tribulations of motherhood.

For eight years they lived the American Dream. In the ninth year of their marriage, it all began to fall apart. Their disbelief at the rapid deterioration of their relationship was undiminished after ten months of conflict. "Here we are, folks! An attractive couple in our early thirties, with apparently everything going for us—two great kids, financial security, no health problems, no in-law problems—we're just too stupid to get along with each other." The tenor of these thoughts reverberated throughout every unguarded moment of their lives.

"This is the pattern again, isn't it?" Ellen asked. She felt as hollow as her voice sounded.

"Yeah. We pick at each other, get in a big fight, separate for a few days, then patch it up so we can start over again. We keep saying we'll be more patient and we mean it at the time, but there's so much anger we can't follow through. Hell, we're trying to push the river back upstream," Rob sighed, weary of the argument.

Ellen's face sagged and she slumped in the chair. Rob sat down across the table, watching her without speaking. He wanted to reach out and run his fingers through her flaxen hair. He didn't. She'd only draw back and he'd feel even more resentment. He thought for a moment of Arthur stroking her hair during lovemaking, then pushed the thought out of his mind. Several months ago, that kind of thinking had nearly driven him crazy but he'd learned to live with it. His own possessiveness had amazed him, yet he couldn't blame her. When things had first started going bad, he'd confided in his secretary; eventually—inevitably, it seemed—they'd had an affair. Ellen found out and turned to Arthur to "regain her self-esteem" as she put it.

During their separations there were more affairs on both sides, but none lasted. Susan was the closest Rob had come to finding someone compatible but there was no joy or excitement in their relationship, only a mutual lust. She was a business associate who had little time for anything but her career. The relationship provided each of them with some companionship and the physical release of sex without commitment.

And now Ellen knew about Susan.

"How long has it been since we've made love to each other, Rob?"

He was startled by the question. "I don't know . . . four or five months, I suppose. You told me you never wanted me to touch you again."

"I know," she replied, so softly he could barely hear her. She looked directly into his eyes. There was no anger in her eyes, only pleading. "I don't understand my feelings or desires, Rob, they're as confused as everything else . . . but I want you. I want you to hold me and I want to feel you inside me. Oh, God, I want you!" she sobbed as he gathered her into his arms in an instinctive gesture of comfort.

"I want you too, baby," he whispered, holding her tightly—shocked at his own eager response. He could feel her uneven breathing on his cheek.

Rob was surprised how light Ellen felt when he picked her up. She often said marital discord was the best diet in the world. As he set her down on the edge of the bed, she smiled uncertainly and touched his face tenderly while he unbuttoned her blouse.

"It was good," he thought when it was over. "I hope it was good for her." He leaned against the headboard, pillow propped behind him, smoking a cigarette. Ellen lay sleeping, her head against his thigh. They hadn't uttered a word but the passion was still there. Their lovemaking was the only positive thing that had transpired between them in months and he became painfully aware of how much he missed her.

The red LEDs on the digital clock radio read 10:30 P.M. At 1:30 A.M., he had smoked half a pack of cigarettes and hadn't moved. "Gotta get some sleep . . . still feel wired, though. Maybe I should use some self-hypnosis." He crushed out the last cigarette and closed his eyes, beginning the familiar, deep breathing he used whenever he wanted to relax. He had learned it at one of the seminars Ellen had talked him into attending.

He started by mentally sending signals to his feet and lower legs. When they felt relaxed, he moved upward, into his upper legs and hips, then into his fingers, hands and lower arms, through the upper arms, then into the back of his neck and shoulder muscles. He could feel the tension draining out of his body.

The induction was next, but instead of going down, he decided to count up into the higher levels of mind, hoping to drift off to sleep in a positive frame of mind.

Soon the induction was complete and he lay without moving for several minutes, expecting to drift away as he lost consciousness. Nothing happened and he realized that his mind was racing as rapidly as ever. "Damn!" he muttered, sitting up and reaching for another cigarette. As the match flared, Rob glimpsed the form of another person out of the corner of his eye— someone was by their dresser! He gasped in surprise and fear but instantly reached for the bedside light and snapped it on.

"What the hell! Who are you and how did you get in here?" he challenged. Sitting in the lotus position atop the dresser was a smiling old man in a dark-blue tunic. Rob glanced at Ellen, surprised that the light and the noise had not disturbed her.

"Don't be afraid, Rob. I mean you no harm."

"How did you get in here?" Rob demanded angrily, moving quickly from the bed toward the old man. He reached out to grab the man by the shoulder and watched dumbfounded as his hand passed through the man's form.

"What the . . ." Rob jumped back in fear. "You're an apparition! You're not even real."

"Oh, I am quite real, I assure you, even though I don't meet your standards of reality."

Rob stood stark naked in a fighting stance a few feet from the smiling figure. The old man appeared to be sixtyish—his short, white beard and lined, weather-beaten face gave Rob an impression of Ernest Hemingway. His tunic fit tightly around the neck; in the dimly lit room, the effect was eerily that of a floating head.

"My name is Solaka, Rob. I'm what your wife would call your 'spirit guide.' I spend a great deal of time with you although you don't realize it consciously."

"I'm not dead, am I?" Rob asked, looking down at his own body for reassurance and becoming aware, for the first time, of his nakedness. "A dream, that's all this is," he mumbled, shaking his head in an attempt to dispel the illusion.

"No," Solaka replied, pointing toward the bed. Rob looked—there he was, in bed beside Ellen, seemingly asleep. "Rob, listen to me for a moment. You are not dead, you are simply out of your physical body. You attained a Higher-Self level of awareness as your body went to sleep, and I thought this would be a good time to assist you to astrally project so we can communicate about your present problems."

"I don't understand," Rob replied disbelievingly.

Solaka continued, "I know you've never taken Ellen's metaphysical interests very seriously, but she has a fairly accurate understanding of a larger reality."

"You mean reincarnation, karma, the other side, and all that stuff?" Rob responded.

"Yes. But right now I'd like to know if you are interested in exploring some potentials that may possibly transform your life. Tonight, the two of you appear to have reached a turning point. You've both given up. At the same time, you're both becoming more fully aware of the love you still share. Now you will move one way or the other. You will separate . . . or begin to rebuild your marriage."

Only the old man's mouth moved. His facial expression was warm and friendly as he continued to sit perfectly still in a yoga posture on top of the dresser.

Rob shook his head. His shoulders hunched, both hands clasped and covering his groin, he stared at the old man in amazement. He no longer felt any fear for his safety, only a nagging suspicion that he might be losing his mind. Things like this didn't happen to businessmen whose creed is hard, cold data and statistics.

"Damn!" he mumbled, thinking that he could use another cigarette but not wanting to turn his back on Solaka. "Okay, sure, I'd like to save my marriage. But neither Ellen nor I seem to be able to get past the anger, the resentment about everything that's happened between us."

"Come with me," Solaka said, holding out his hand. Rob hesitated and looked around the room. At the very moment he decided he had nothing to lose by playing along, he had an impression of movement . . . without accompanying physical feelings of movement. Blackness became flashes of light that faded into blackness again before coalescing into a room filled, floor to ceiling, with electronic equipment—video monitors, sound systems, and computers.

"Is this for real?" Rob asked as his shrewd businessman's eyes inventoried and estimated the equipment's worth.

"No, not as you perceive reality, Rob, but it will serve you as well. Ellen has spoken to you in the past about karma—cause and effect. Now is not the time to explore the subject in philosophical detail, but I will tell you that reincarnation and karma are the basis of reality on the physical plane. And you and Ellen have shared many prior lifetimes."

Rob looked at Solaka without comment.

Solaka continued, "In the memory banks of your subconscious mind is a memory of everything you have ever experienced, Rob. Every thought, every word, every deed—*everything* you have ever experienced is recorded . . . forever. This equipment can transfer your forgotten memories to these screens. Look at that monitor—there are you and Ellen in Mesopotamia. It was your first lifetime together and you were part of the Sumerian settlement."

"Oh, come on," Rob said, looking at what appeared to be a television sitcom with two strange-looking people. Both were short and stocky with long, narrow heads. Rob turned to Solaka. "I feel like Scrooge watching "Saturday Night Live" with the Ghost of Christmas Past. This is ridiculous!"

"What do you have to lose, Rob?"

"Nothing, I suppose. If that's Ellen and me on the screen, what are we doing?"

"Harvesting dates. You were the male in that lifetime too, Rob . . . and the two of you didn't get along very well then, either."

As Rob watched, the larger Sumerian struck the other. The female struck back, and they were yelling and scuffling as the scene flickered out. "That was approximately 3300 B.C. The next lifetime you shared was in Persia, 550 B.C. You were both male in that lifetime, comrades-in-arms in the service of Cyrus the Great."

The screen illuminated once more. Rob watched as two young men, probably in their late twenties, strolled through a street in Babylon. The friendly scene faded into another in which the men were vying for the attentions of a beautiful young woman. The scene ended as one of the men drew a sword and ran it through the stomach of the other.

"You both wanted the same woman in that life, Rob. In a fit of rage, Ellen killed you."

Rob turned from the screen and faced Solaka. "Oh, that's just great!" he spat.

"You balanced that in Constantinople in A.D. 332 when you condemned Ellen to a life of servitude to a cruel master." New images appeared on the screen.

"This is beginning to look like a Cecil B. DeMille epic," Rob thought to himself as he attempted to identify with the images flickering before him. "Have we ever managed to get along?" he wondered aloud.

"Oh, yes, a little better each incarnation since the lifetime Ellen killed you in Persia. You have reincarnated together nine times, the last life in Japan at the turn of the century. Would you like to see more?"

"No," Rob replied. "I can't really relate to these movies as being Ellen and me. So what? Even if what you're telling me is true, so what?"

"So, you're going to keep reincarnating together until you get it right, Rob, until you finally come to understand that love, not fear, is the path to liberation. You can resolve it in this life or you can postpone it until a future lifetime. Would you like me to begin at the beginning and explain things very basically?"

"Very basically," Rob emphasized, nodding his head and raising his hands in a gesture of confusion.

"Before you were born into your present life, Rob, you existed in the nonphysical realms on the fourth of seven levels. The vibrational rate of each level becomes more intense as you ascend. The first level is the *physical plane* upon which you currently experience existence. The second is the *astral plane*, the third is the *mental plane*, the fourth is the *creative plane*, the fifth is the *spiritual intelligence plane*, the sixth is the *spiritual wisdom plane*, and the seventh is the *Godhead*.

"To make it easier to understand, let's say that the astral plane exists as a vibration between 100 and 200," Solaka continued. "The mental plane exists as a vibration between 200 and 300, the creative plane between a vibration of 300 and 400. And so on, with each level increasing in vibration.

"You were born with a vibrational rate of 362. That's the rate you'd earned as a result of the way you've lived your past lives—lifetimes with and without Ellen. You can also raise your vibrational rate through your own efforts on the other side, but it can be done much faster on the physical plane. By punching into this computer, I can see that you have been living this lifetime with a lot of negativity. Your current vibrational rate has slipped to 358. While that's not a big drop, you're obviously going the wrong way. If you died today, you'd find yourself back on the fourth level on the other side."

"Good God, Solaka. If I'm really on the other side, in spirit, I can't imagine that you have or need computers."

"Rob, this is to communicate with you in a manner you will understand by using forms you are familiar with. Instead, let's assume that your lifetime is being recorded by little green men who etch your progress onto great gold pillars in heaven." The familiar surroundings of the room with electronic equipment began to fade and golden pillars began to form. Little elves with hammers and chisels were hard at work, doing exactly as Solaka had described.

"Got it! I'll stick with the computers and television monitors," Rob said, rubbing his temples. "Just out of curiosity," he continued, "what if, when I die and cross over to the other side, I don't like the fourth level and decide to climb up to the fifth level?"

"Even if you could, Rob, you wouldn't be able to tolerate the more intense vibration of the fifth level. And you wouldn't want to go down to the third level because it is much less desirable."

"I take it my goal is to reach the Godhead?" Rob asked.

"The goal of everyone on the physical and non-physical planes is to return to the Godhead. Most physical entities don't realize this consciously, but subconsciously they are drawn to perfection."

"But I've been living sinfully, reducing my vibrational rate?" Rob asked sarcastically.

"Sin has nothing to do with it, Rob. Everything you think, say or do, creates karma that is harmonious, neutral or disharmonious. You've been expressing a lot of disharmony in your life. Everything you experience is a test. Big or small, every situation is an opportunity to respond . . . in one way or another. The physical plane is a classroom offering you continual opportunities to test your level of awareness. 'Level of awareness' is another way to say 'vibrational rate.' When you respond with positive thoughts, love or compassion, or in some situations with neutrality, you're probably passing the tests. When you respond with negative thoughts—spite, anger, blame, desire to control others, or desire for revenge—you are probably failing your tests and generating disharmonious karma."

"Well, I guess I must admit to being a bit negative lately." Rob started to laugh, then stopped, wondering if it were appropriate.

Solaka smiled. "Rob, before you were born, you sat down with me and others much wiser than I, to decide upon the major tests you would encounter in your current incarnation. Would you like to see and hear some of that meeting?"

Another screen flickered, then became illuminated, displaying an overhead view of an iridescent white room. In the center was a large, round table with a small circular area cut out of one edge. Within this smaller circle was an entity whom Rob perceived only as a glowing light.

"Is that me?" Rob asked, pointing to the light within the small circle. Surrounding the table were seven more entities of light.

Solaka nodded. "Listen with your mind, Rob."

"Now, let's proceed to the next question." The voice seemed to emanate from the brightest light. "Are you ready to explore another physical incarnation with Alna?"

"Yes, I am. We made much progress during the Japanese lifetime. And, since then, we've been working together in spirit to refine our love. I feel we can experience a relationship of minimal negativity with a very good potential for harmony."

"Does Alna also agree to another shared incarnation?"

"Yes."

"Then it shall be."

The screen flickered and faded. "Alna is Ellen's soul name. It offers a vibration that is unique in the universe," Solaka explained. "What you have just observed is a meeting that takes place between an entity soon to be incarnated on the physical plane, and the Lords of Karma. The final choice is always left up to you, but the elders will offer suggestions and then arrange the logistics of the soon-to-be-experienced lifetime. It must be arranged for you to meet the people required to resolve your karma."

"What if I'd chosen a lifetime of perfect harmony, fame, and lots of easy money?" Rob asked.

"You wouldn't be allowed to experience anything you hadn't earned," Solaka said. "Besides, from a spiritual perspective, your goal is always to evolve, so you choose those lessons you most need to learn."

"What about someone like Elvis Presley, who attained incredible fame and fortune?" Rob continued, now interested.

"Fame and wealth are karmic rewards . . . but they are also tests. Elvis must decide himself as to how he used his gifts. Were they used to help others or were they used entirely for self-pleasure? He will be his own judge and jury, and his next incarnation will reflect his needed learning, just as with everyone else."

"Were you one of those light beings sitting around the table, Solaka?"

"No, oh, no! They were the seven Lords of Karma. Because you and I agreed that I would serve as your spiritual guide in this life, I was allowed to attend the meeting, but I was sitting off to the side."

"Well, judging from the last several months, Ellen and I certainly haven't lived up to our own spiritual expectations, have we?" Rob said, again staring at the blank monitor screen. He sighed loudly.

"Maybe not, Rob, but you carried into this lifetime the intuitive awareness necessary to make your relationship with Ellen successful. You also carried with you selfish desires to have things your way, and carnal desires that, when allowed to remain unchecked, have not served you.

"From the beginning, you and Ellen have picked at each other in little ways. You both attempted to change the other to be who and what you wanted your mate to be. At first, neither of you really minded, but, over the years, the little irritations became larger irritations and the disagreements became major issues."

"You're right about that," Rob responded. "It seems like the anger just slowly grew until it was out of control. Our pride was hurt and we became angrier and angrier with each other. It wasn't always apparent on the surface, but underneath . . . whew! We just waited for the opportunity to lash out verbally, to withhold emotions, or to irritate each other. And that opportunity came along . . . again and again! Then it turned to detachment. Ellen became so cold that I turned to another woman. I said I didn't want Ellen to find out, but subconsciously I think I did. I probably wanted to hurt her. I felt frustrated—I wanted to say, 'Look, stupid, you don't love me the way I need to be loved, but this beautiful woman over here does. Look, I'm desirable! Why don't you realize it?' I wanted to rub it in, I suppose."

"And Ellen was doing the same thing, Rob," Solaka said.

"Oh, I know, I know. But so what? What's done is done. And if you're right about this metaphysical stuff, the anger relates back a lot farther than this life. Maybe I'm still trying to get Ellen for killing me in Babylon, and she's still pissed off about being a slave."

"You're getting the idea, Rob. Eventually, you'll both rise above your subconscious fear programming. You are capable of it now, but you also have the free will to extend the suffering. You could probably go on for twenty or thirty more lifetimes, until you fully realize, on a soul level, that what you are doing isn't working."

"Is everyone who marries destined to remain together for an entire lifetime?" Rob asked. "If so, there are a lot of souls flunking their tests."

"No, not everyone is destined to be together throughout an entire lifetime. Each situation is different. Some souls have arranged to part once they reach a certain point in their relationship. Others are destined to interact with more than one mate. But in each case involving separation, the goal is always to part positively, with compassion and without creating any further disharmonious karma."

"What about Ellen and me? How did we set it up?"

"There is no other mate waiting in the wings for either of you, Rob."

"But what will happen if Ellen and I decide to get a divorce? Will we both remain single for the rest of our lives?"

"Not necessarily. That will be up to you. If you divorce, you could decide to put off any further relationship learning until your next life. If you do, there are plenty of other lessons you could work on. They might not be particularly desirable from your perspective, but from the viewpoint of soul growth, all lessons need to be learned.

"But let's say that, after a year or so of being single, Rob, you are attracted to another woman and the two of you enter into a relationship. No matter what the relationship appears to be on the surface, the woman will have a karmic configuration matching your own. You might or might not be dealing with the same lessons you've encountered with Ellen, but the opportunity to learn more about relationships is assured."

"So, the bottom line is, I can try to work it out

with Ellen, or I'll end up working on growth lessons anyway, whether alone or with someone else? Is that what you're saying?"

"Basically," Solaka replied.

"Even if I were to exert superhuman effort, I don't know that Ellen would respond. For several months, I've felt we were beyond the point of no return."

"There are no guarantees, Rob. But what do you have to lose?"

"Tonight, I realized how much I missed her," Rob replied thoughtfully. His voice was warm, remembering their lovemaking earlier that evening. "But where would I start, Solaka?"

"I don't know, Rob. Where *would* you start? I am your guide. I'm always there for you on the other side. I'm the intuitive voice in your mind that encourages you to be positive, to resolve your karma. But I can't tell you what to do. I can encourage you when you're on the right track and I can inspire you to do better, but to tell you directly what to do would be for me to take on your karma."

"Why do you serve as my guide, Solaka?"

"To repay a debt. You were once my guide . . . and a pretty good one, I might add. Also, it is a way for me to advance myself—to increase my own vibrational rate while in spirit."

"Thanks. It looks like I need all the help I can get, huh? When Ellen and I first met, there were no negatives. Today, to start over would be twice as hard as starting from scratch."

Solaka shook his head. "The history, myths, legends, and fairy tales of mankind are filled with stories of love found, love lost, love regained, and love transformed. You and Ellen have the potential to transform your love."

"This may sound funny, but what you're saying sounds just like what was said in a seminar I attended once with Ellen. I didn't want to go but I was willing to do anything to help rebuild our relationship. The only thing I got out of it, though, was learning a self-hypnosis technique."

"I am aware of the situation," Solaka said. "It was the technique you learned there that enabled you to go into your Higher Self tonight and contact me. And who do you think influenced you to attend the seminar?"

"You even get involved in things like that?" Rob was surprised. "It's so complicated," he sighed.

"Not really, Rob. Karma is a system of total justice. As you sow, so shall you reap. And you get as many chances as you need to win . . . to let go of fear and to learn to express unconditional love in response to everyone and everything."

"Okay," Rob said, nodding his head. "I have to admit that I like the idea of total justice. But, regarding my relationship with Ellen—I want to let go of the anger. How do I let go of the anger?"

"By understanding anger, Rob, and by acting. Karma *means* action. Anger is a fear-based emotion and a protection against pain. You suppress your pain with anger but in doing so you create a bondage, because you accumulate more anger, until it builds into a rage that lies just below the surface. With the slightest provocation, it explodes. To *repress* anger is disharmonious. To *express* anger is disharmonious. Only by *understanding* anger can you begin to rise above anger.

"The next time you find yourself beginning to get angry at Ellen, remind yourself that there are only two possible reasons for the anger. You either want her approval and she isn't giving it to you, or you want to control her and she isn't allowing you to. Neither approval nor control are your rights. Your expectations are creating the anger—expectations in conflict with what is."

Rob was silent for a while. "I guess you're right, Solaka. I was just thinking about some of our recent fights. In each case, when Ellen didn't live up to my expectations, I became angry. Obviously, what you're saying is true, but it will take more than simply understanding it. We need to communicate and compromise and come up with some new agreements."

"Think back to the seminar, Rob. There was a lecture about changing your behavior and a process was given to enable you to effect the changes. Do you remember?"

"Yes, vaguely."

"The idea is to be willing to make immediate sacrifices for long-term satisfaction. You don't have to change how you feel about something to affect it *if* you are willing to change what you are doing. If your behavior creates disharmony, change it. Immediate changes in behavior will lead to very real changes in attitude—which, in turn, can lead to fulfillment of your needs."

"That's the bottom line, isn't it? Fulfillment of our needs. My needs haven't been fulfilled nor have Ellen's for a very long time."

"Everyone on the physical plane has two psychological needs," Solaka explained. "The need to love and be loved, and the need to feel worthwhile, to yourself and to others. You and Ellen have had very unrealistic expectations of each other. Yes, you want her love and she wants your love, but love is an involuntary reaction based in part upon how you treat each other. And it isn't up to your wife to build your self-esteem. Self-esteem is the result of what you do. When you do things that cause you to feel badly about yourself, you lower your self-esteem and your vibrational rate as well."

"I can accept that."

"It's time to return now, Rob."

"Don't I get to take a tour with the ghosts of Christmas Present and Christmas Future?" Rob asked. He was barely able to keep the laughter from his voice.

"Your future isn't written," Solaka replied with a big smile which began to fade into the blackness and the flashing lights.

"Wait a minute, Solaka. I want to ask some more questions!"

"I'm never far away—just listen to your inner thoughts." His voice was fading and there was only blackness.

With a gasp, Rob's body jerked wide awake and he sat up. He was sweating. The room remained the same. Ellen lay beside him, sound asleep. The bedside lamp was on and the red LEDs on the digital clock glowed 3:05 A.M. "A dream, that's all it was, just a dream," he said to himself, and as he spoke, the red numbers on the clock face flickered and faded away.

Rob and Ellen Bradwick attended a seminar I conducted in the Pacific Northwest. A few months later, Rob sent me a nineteen-page letter describing his relationship with his wife and the experience with Solaka which he wanted me to comment upon. He explained that the clock actually "burned out" at that moment, and they had to purchase a new clock radio.

I responded with a quick note explaining that I had heard of several similar encounters, and in my opinion, it was probably a valid out-of-body experience.

I suggested he take the experience very seriously and added that I would call in a few months to see how they were doing. Three months later, I made good on my commitment. "What's happened since your visit with Solaka?" I asked.

"I still don't know if it was a dream, an out-of-body experience, or a hallucination, but whatever it was, it certainly changed my life," Rob replied. "I've been approaching my life and my relationship from a transformed perspective and it seems to be working. It was hard at first, but now Ellen and I are getting along just great. She slowly began to respond to the 'new' me in a new way. Now I think she's more positive than I am.

"We take the time to do something together every day, even if it's just taking a short walk. We communicate freely now. We also have our own interests which we pursue. Ellen has begun publishing a small paper that she can produce at home. It's a local children's activities calendar, and she sells advertising to support it. Sometimes things still get touchy, and maybe it's too soon to tell, but I think we're going to make it."

"Have you told Ellen about the experience with Solaka?" I asked.

"Not yet," he replied. "If you're going to write about it, I think I'll just let her read the story in your book."

4

Cause and Its Effect on Marcie McGyver

The Camaro Z28 sideslipped across the yellow line as Marcie McGyver downshifted into one of the tightest curves on Mulholland. "I've taken it better a thousand times before," she thought, rubbing her burning eyes, still red and puffy from crying.

Before she left the hypnotist's office, he had given her an audiocassette of the entire session, including the preceding interview as well as the past-life regression. Her voice filled the car as she played back the last few hours of her life on the car stereo. "Instant déjà vu," she thought wildly.

"Gwen Thornton suggested I see you," she heard herself saying. "I believe you've seen her on several occasions."

"Yes, I always enjoy working with Gwen," replied Dr. Milton Edric. "I sometimes think I get more out of our sessions than she does. I must thank her for the recommendation. Now, how can I be of service to you, Marcie?"

"Well, I'm new at exploring metaphysical approaches to problems, but I've read that every feeling we have relates back to a cause—either an event or a series of events in our past. Gwen is convinced that it can even relate back to events that occurred in past lives. Regression has helped her understand the conflict she was having with one of her children. The experience changed her perspective of the relationship and the situation really improved."

Dr. Edric had been seated behind a large mahogany desk; his office was tastefully decorated and gave one a comfortable, secure feeling. Marcie remembered thinking how his bald head stood out against the high-backed, black leather chair. She'd expected someone with deep hypnotic eyes, wearing a turtleneck sweater and a weird occult necklace. Instead, the good doctor seemed more like her dentist than Svengali. His manner, though informal, was completely professional, and she felt comfortable and perfectly at ease with him.

"Tell me about your problem, Marcie."

"I'm preoccupied with death, Doctor. I never used to be . . . until I met my husband. When I first met Robert, it was incredible. I had been married before but was single for more than two years when mutual friends introduced us at a car show at the L.A. Convention Center. When Robert looked at me the first time, I just melted—I couldn't even respond. He was the man I had waited for all my life . . . and there he was, in the flesh. I was scared and excited. Later, he admitted he had the same reaction."

Marcie switched her attention from the tape to the road as brake lights flashed on the cars ahead of her. Pulling to a stop at the red light on Topanga, she tapped her fingers on the gearshift, thinking about the tape as it continued playing in the background. "Best damned marketing tactic I've ever seen," she thought. "He gives you a tape of the interview and your past-life regression, and you play it for everyone patient enough to listen. That's how I ended up in his office—after listening to a tape of Gwen's regression, I had to experience it myself."

Marcie turned right and was soon in Gwen's neighborhood located in the heart of Woodland Hills. Gwen's BMW was parked in the driveway of the large, Spanish-style stucco house. "Bastardized Spanish with a little Mount Vernon thrown in," was the way Gwen described her "humble abode." Marcie and Gwen had met in college and became the best of friends; they had maintained that friendship ever since. Both were now thirty-seven but each could still pass for thirty. Keeping "fit, trim, and firm" was a joint concern that occupied a large share of their conversations. Gwen claimed to be jealous of Marcie's lean but well-rounded, 108-pound body and Marcie said she'd trade it for Gwen's flowing, jet-black hair and smooth olive complexion.

"You've been crying," Gwen exclaimed in alarm as she opened the door. She put her arm around Marcie and pulled her into the house.

"Oh, I'm fine . . . *now*," Marcie replied, emphasizing the last word. "It was a pretty emotional experience at the time—past-life regression can ruin your makeup."

Gwen laughed. "I can't wait to hear every detail," she said. "Sit down and I'll get us some coffee."

"Well, here it is, every single word," Marcie said, laying the two cassette tapes on the coffee table as she sank back into the comfortable overstuffed couch. "I just realized what a great advertising technique it is to give your patients tapes of their sessions."

"That's true, but there's more to it than that,"

Gwen said, handing Marcie a steaming cup of the specialty of the house—cappuccino à la Gwen. "I'm sure hypnotists may have problems with an occasional woman who projects an erotic, altered-state experience, and then thinks it really happened with the doctor. So, the tape is his insurance. If you were in his office for two hours, both you and he have recordings of the entire session and he is covered because his assistant logged you in and out. He can also prove that he didn't give you advice you could blame him for later."

"Got it," Marcie said, tilting her head to the side and smiling. "But I think an erotic episode would have been more fun than what I just went through. I've been listening to the pre-regression interview in the car. It just covers my explanation of my problem—of being so damned afraid that I'm going to die or Robert is going to die, or that something dreadful will happen to take away our wonderful relationship and life together. You're familiar with all that and you've heard Dr. Edric's preparation talk before. Here, the second tape covers the regression itself," Marcie said, handing the tape to Gwen.

Dr. Milton Edric's soothing voice filled the living room from all four sides as it was amplified through Gwen's powerful stereo system. "We now begin to work together to bring forgotten awareness to the surface so that you may better understand that which influences, restricts or motivates you in the present. It is time to let go of the physical and open to your memories of an event in your past that has programmed you to fear death . . . or separation from your husband, Robert. You may go back to an earlier time in your present life, or you may return to an event that transpired in a previous incarnation. You are relaxed and at ease, in a deep hypnotic sleep, and I am going to count backward from five to one. On the count of one, vivid impressions will begin to flow into your mind, impressions from your past that relate to the cause we seek to understand. . . ."

As Marcie sat on the couch, listening to the tape of Dr. Edric's voice counting backward, she clutched her coffee cup tightly with both hands and closed her eyes.

"You are now there and impressions are beginning to come in. Vivid impressions, and when you can, I want you to speak up and tell me what you see and what you are doing."

There was silence except for the faint sound of heavy breathing and a slight tape hiss. It seemed to last for minutes. Then a thin female voice said, "I'm watching a wedding festival winding slowly through the streets. The bride's face is covered with a lace veil, and her dress is made of lace. She is carrying beautiful red flowers. Her husband is laughing. He looks so proud and so do all the others. Some are young and some are old. I hear music—a flute . . . no, two flutes and a funny drum, and a woman dressed in purple is hitting her hips with a tambourine."

"Who are you? You are one of those people you're observing. I want you to tell me who you are," said Dr. Edric.

"I'm the bride," Marcie said, very softly.

In the pause that followed her last words, Gwen blurted out, "Boy, that sure doesn't sound like you, Marcie!"

Holding one hand to her throat with an expression of anxiety, Marcie nodded silently in agreement.

The tape continued. "Tell me more about this," Dr. Edric said. "I want to know the name of the country you are now in."

"Portugal."

"Can you tell me the year?"

"Of course! It is 1470—why don't you know that?"

"I'm a stranger here. Tell me, please, who rules Portugal?"

"Ferdinand of Aragon and Isabella of Castile. They were married last year."

"What is your name?"

"Maria, and my husband's name is Philip. Do you see the beautiful ship sailing into the harbor?"

"Oh, yes. What city are you in now, Maria?"

"Lisbon, of course. My, my."

Marcie couldn't help smiling as she listened to the words, remembering the scene she had seen with her inner eyes—a wedding party of happy people winding down a small street overlooking a busy harbor, the sun shining and puffy clouds crowding a bright blue sky as music filled the air. As she listened to her taped response to the questions, she realized how completely she had become Maria during the regression. Marcie didn't exist. The questions confused her because she hadn't known where they were coming from, but she answered anyway, interjecting an occasional, bemused, "my, my."

"All right, Maria. I want you to let go of this and move forward in time to something very important that will happen in your future. You will remember everything you are observing, but on the count of three, time will have passed and something very important will be about to happen. One, two, three. You are now there. What do you see and what . . ."

Before he could finish the question, there was the harsh, ragged sound of air being rapidly inhaled. Then, a terrible scream filled the room.

Marcie shivered and shut her eyes again, quickly placing the coffee cup on the table to keep from spilling it. Gwen stared at Marcie while her face mirrored her shock.

"Men! Dirty men! Ugh . . . sailors, I think. Three of them—they have me behind a building. They dragged me here and they are forcing me to . . . Oh, God, oh, God. I'm screaming and screaming. The one with the white beard is hitting me in the face. 'Shut yer yap,' he keeps saying, 'shut yer yap, shut yer yap.' Oh, God, my face is splitting open, he's hitting me so hard, and one of the others is sticking his thing in me."

"You are experiencing no physical pain, but I want you to speak up and tell me everything that is happening," Dr. Edric's voice was soothing and comforting.

"There's nothing more to tell. I'm lying there, but I seem to be floating above myself. I look awful. My clothes are all torn off and I can't even recognize my face. Oh, God! Where is Philip? Where is Philip? I hate those men! I hate them, I hate them!" The voice was loud and angry. As Marcie listened to her voice sobbing on the tape, she realized she was crying along with herself.

"You were dead, weren't you?" Gwen asked, as the voice on the tape sobbed wildly.

"Yes," Marcie answered, her voice choked with grief.

"I hate them!!!" screamed Marcie's taped voice, reliving the five-hundred-year-old anguish.

Gwen snapped off the cassette tape. "Maybe you don't want to go through all this again right now?" Her voice was concerned.

"No, it's all right, Gwen. Dr. Edric explained that I wouldn't have become so emotional if the experience weren't still affecting me. Later in the session, he directed me up to a Higher-Self level where I explained that Philip is Robert in this life. In Portugal, we had only been married for three months before the rape and murder. I had loved him so much and he was taken away from me before we had even begun to have a life. It created a soul-level phobia that was triggered in this life when I met Robert. Dr. Edric called it 'false-fear karma.' The fear isn't valid in the context of my current life, but it's charged with so much psychic energy, it bleeds through. I guess my subconscious programming is out of alignment with my conscious reality."

"Does Edric think this will help you to stop dwelling on the fear?" Gwen asked.

"Yes. He says false-fear karma is the easiest to overcome. I had never completely experienced the situation so he made me relive it without the physical pain. When I had crossed over into death in that life, I was still angry and upset, crying out for Philip. I hadn't released it, and this evidently assured that I would carry the effect forward."

"Shall I turn the tape back on?" Gwen asked.

"Oh, sure, Gwen, but run it forward a bit. Actually, the best part is yet to come. Dr. Edric explained that it is quite unusual to follow a subject very far into death, but he kept asking questions and I kept answering them, so he just kept going."

Marcie's voice came out of the speakers just as she finished. The effect was so odd that Gwen and Marcie looked at each other and burst into hysterical laughter. After they calmed down, Marcie said, "No, run it a bit farther, please." Gwen pushed the fast-forward button.

"That was part of my reintroduction to the world of spirit. After you die, you experience a rest period where you have a chance to meet with all the people you knew while you were on earth in physical form— old friends from many lifetimes. Then you review your entire physical lifetime to see what you learned and what you still need to learn. They explained that in a previous incarnation I had been a soldier who killed a man in front of his wife and children. Evidently, the fastest way to learn karmically is to directly experience the consequences of your actions. As Maria, I wanted to remain and enjoy my lifetime with Philip but I wasn't allowed to do so because I needed to experience the pain of having a loving relationship cut short, as I had cut that man's short."

"And to learn the value of life," Gwen said so softly, Marcie could barely hear her. Gwen pushed the play button again.

It was Dr. Edric's voice. "What is the entity saying to you, Marcie?"

"He says that I'm free to rest or attend classes or be of service. To rest means that I can do anything I want to do—I have only to think of an environment or situation and it becomes my reality. If I want to walk through beautiful apple orchards, I am there, and the apples are ripe and delicious. If I wish to be dressed in a beautiful gown, dancing at a royal ball for the Queen of Spain, I am there, and it is as real as any physical experience."

"Can you tell me about attending classes?" Dr. Edric asked.

"They aren't classes as you would think of classes. They take place in beautiful gardens and airy, shimmering structures. A teacher is there, and anyone who wants to listen or participate is welcome. I was told that we are each free to choose how we appear to others. We can choose the appearance of our last physical life if we wish—that is what most do. Or we are free to create any appearance that suits us. But there is no ego here, so we do not make ourselves beautiful out of vanity. We make ourselves beautiful because beauty is perfection, and perfection is an attribute of the God-head. Everyone wears white togas or loose, flowing white garments."

"What are you going to do?"

"I want to be of service; I have been assigned to assist souls as they cross over into spirit from the physical plane."

"How do you do that?"

"I am about to help someone right now. There is a terrible battle going on below me. There are many of us waiting on this side; we have each been assigned to assist one soul to make the transition."

"Is it predestined who will live and who will die in this battle?" Dr. Edric's voice was no longer inquiring in a detached, impartial manner. It conveyed his obviously sincere interest in her answer.

"When death is this close, it is destined," she replied. "My assignment probably isn't a day over seventeen and he's scared to death, but he isn't shirking from his duty. He charges along as bravely as men twice his age."

"What is happening now?" asked Dr. Edric.

"Men, fighting and dying. Some try to hide but there is no place to hide. Some have fallen down and lie crying in the mud, unhurt except in their minds. They fight with swords and crude muskets, without even knowing the reason for which they fight and die. And we watch and wait, knowing we can do nothing but send them light and love. Those who have chosen to die here need this experience to balance something in their past. My young man needs to learn about the futility of violence, but if he dies with hatred toward his enemies, he will have to go through it again in a future life in similar circumstances."

Marcie walked across the room to the stereo and pushed the cassette player's stop button. "Gwen, all this is coming out of the mouth of someone who knows next to nothing about the metaphysical world. Everything I know has come from our discussions, and we've never talked about anything like this."

"Well, you've sure got my attention," Gwen responded. "Turn it back on."

The tape started again. "He's hit! He's hit!" Marcie heard her voice saying, and she recalled how she had seen the images in her mind. A bullet had entered the young man's stomach and he fell, face first, into the mud. With his last remaining strength, he managed to pull his face out of the muck, gasping and wheezing as his body fought to continue breathing. Tears mixed with the mud and his whimpers were drowned by the roar of the battle. The moment he fell, she had been drawn to his side, telepathically sending comforting thoughts. "Your mother is over here, Paul, you'll see her soon. She loves you. She loves you and I love you. We all love you." His ragged breathing caught, and he seemed to shiver all over as he accepted his fate. His head relaxed as his body slumped into the muddy earth. It was over.

Long moments passed and only the sound of tape hiss filled the living room. "What's happening?" Gwen demanded. "Why aren't you saying anything?"

"I was experiencing it in my mind," Marcie replied, "but I guess Dr. Edric didn't know what to ask after that. Damn, look at me, I'm crying again. What a morning!" She wiped her eyes with a handkerchief as her mind returned to the scenes of the dying boy. "He didn't know what had happened. At first, I had quite a time convincing him that he was dead. He saw his body lying in the bloody mud but he still couldn't accept it until his mother appeared. Then he was joyful. I don't know how else to say it, just joyful. He said it was a relief to be dead and he wasn't cold any more."

"Then what happened?" Gwen asked, her hands making unconscious "keep the story rolling" gestures in the air.

Marcie laughed. "Then Dr. Edric brought me back to the present time and gave me a lot of positive suggestions about letting go of my fears and remembering everything I had just experienced. Before awakening me, he suggested I would have dreams about the regression experiences and awaken tomorrow morning with additional awareness. And that's it."

"Whew!" Gwen sighed, sinking back into the couch cushions.

"If, back in Portugal, I was killed three months after we were married, it seems Robert would at least have some anxiety about losing me again," Marcie said, looking directly at Gwen with a puzzled expression.

"Not necessarily. Both of you had different past-life backgrounds before your Portuguese incarnation. Maybe he was able to resolve the loss in the years following Maria's death. You crossed over into spirit filled with anger and hatred, so you had no earth time to work through it. Robert/Philip could also have been karmically devastated but worked it out in other incarnations between that life and this one."

"Wouldn't I, too, have had other incarnations in the last five hundred years?" Marcie asked doubtfully.

"Probably, but you may not have been willing to deal with this particular karmic programming until now. Maybe you didn't feel you had the strength until now. And maybe you set it up so that you would be introduced to metaphysics before attempting to deal with it in this life."

"You mean I was predestined to meet you in college and later have you introduce me to this awareness, just so I could work through an issue I didn't even know I had until I met my husband-to-be?" Marcie laughed incredulously.

Gwen shrugged.

"That's pretty far out, Gwen. I don't know if I buy that."

"I know it sounds far out, but if everything is karmic, then maybe it isn't such a wild idea after all. I think that karma is the basis of reality. We either evolved from a cell in the sea, becoming what we are over millions of years and there is no greater meaning to life . . . or there is some kind of plan. If there is a plan, it would follow that there is an intelligence behind the plan. If that's so, it seems to me that it would also follow that justice would be part of the plan. Karma is a science/religion/philosophy of total justice. It explains all the pain and suffering in the world."

"But I believe in evolution, Gwen. How can you deny the scientific evidence?"

"I believe the probability of evolution too, Marcie, but not *just* evolution. Yeah, I'm sure that evolution is how man got here, but I think that when mankind reached a certain point in his evolutionary progress, souls began crossing over from the spiritual side to inhabit those bodies and explore physical reality."

"Why would a soul do that, Gwen?"

"Maybe as an experiment, but in our physical forms we interacted with 'intention,' creating karma that ties us to the earth until it is resolved. In other words, maybe we entrapped ourselves. Of course, there are hundreds of other possibilities as well, Marcie."

"All I know is that, whatever it amounts to, if I have less anxiety about losing Robert, it's going to be a great relief and well worth the effort."

"For your husband as well," Gwen laughed. "Now maybe you can let him go out of town on a business trip without making him promise to call you every ninety minutes."

Marcie and Robert McGyver attended one of my three-day psychic seminars in Sedona several months after Marcie's past-life regression with Dr. Edric. Sedona, Arizona, is the location of four energy vortexes which amplify an individual's psychic energy, usually assisting participants to be more psychic than they normally are.

On Saturday afternoon, the second day of the seminar, the participants are free to explore the energy vortexes on their own. My wife, Tara, and I were sitting by the Poco Diablo Resort pool watching our children swim, when Marcie and Robert approached and asked if they could talk to us for a few minutes.

Robert was a tall man, at least 6'2", and very handsome; he was probably in his mid-forties. Standing beside him, Marcie appeared much smaller than her 5'3". They made a striking couple and were obviously very much in love. Dressed conservatively for the Arizona mountains, Robert opened the conversation by apologizing. "I thought all this stuff was for true-believer types," he said meekly. "If it weren't for my wife, this is the last place I'd ever be. But I can't deny what I've experienced."

"You're Richard's favorite kind of seminar participant," Tara said, a trace of laughter in her voice.

Marcie could hardly contain her delight. "Robert was being a good sport, determined to be supportive of his wacko wife and have a nice, three-day vacation at the same time. He had planned to spend it sitting by the pool and hiking through the red rocks, but I persuaded him to attend the seminar and participate in the telepathy session. I couldn't believe it—he was much better than I at sending and receiving telepathic messages and symbols. During the clairvoyant session, we both saw visions but it was the automatic writing experiment that really did him in."

"My hand took off all on its own and wrote two full pages of communications," Robert said earnestly, as if I would be surprised.

"That's what it was supposed to do, Robert," I laughed. "At least 190 out of the 200 people in the ballroom received automatic writing this morning and now they are hopefully receiving more in the vortexes."

"We're going to go to Boynton Canyon in a little while," Robert continued. "But, first, we wanted to ask your opinion about some things."

Marcie described her past-life experience as Maria, then flipped open a notebook which she handed to me. "This is what Robert received in automatic writing this morning. Would you take just a moment to read it, please?"

I love to teach automatic writing; most people, when properly prepared, are successful on the first or second attempt. Two directed sessions are part of the seminar, and in this particular experiment, I had asked the participants to choose someone they would like to contact who had once lived on earth. I usually suggest that they choose a wise soul, explaining that even if the soul had incarnated, the energy remains and they can communicate from a superconscious level of mind. I instruct the participants to write the name of the individual they desire to contact at the top of the page, and a question they want answered beneath it. The heading in Robert's handbook read: "My Father, Jonathan R. McGyver." Beneath that was the question, "How have you been since you died?"

The writing below was markedly different from that of the heading. It read: "Hello again, Scooch! You think this is silly and would prefer to ignore looking for any deeper meanings in life, so your old man is going to have to shake you up one more time. Remember when you lost your wallet a couple of months ago? You cancelled all your credit cards and spent days filling out applications for new ones, getting a new driver's license, and all the rest of the hassle. Well, my boy, your wallet fell out of your pants pocket into your old hiking boots at the bottom of your closet. It's still there, in the left boot. And if that is so, maybe the rest of what I have to say is valid. Marcie is beginning to understand the true meaning of manifest existence, and in turn, she is to teach you. The two of you have been together in many lifetimes. You are soulmates and your relationship is an earned reward which you must value if you wish to project it into future incarnations. By value I mean to cherish, and I also mean that you must equally increase vibrationally or you will be separated in future lives. At this time, Marcie is advancing her level of awareness more rapidly than you are. Listen to her. Love, Dad. P.S. Your mother sends her love. We are often with you when your body is in deep sleep but you don't consciously remember it."

Robert tilted back in his chair and looked at me. "Sounds like a hokey letter from home, doesn't it? Only, we have someone house-sitting for us in California. I called and asked the woman to check my hiking boots. The wallet was there and I'm a mental basket case." His bearing was stiff and proud, but his dark eyes showed the dullness of disbelief.

"I think you're in very good hands," Tara said, flashing a wide smile at Marcie.

Marcie pointed to the line of automatic writing that said, ". . . you must both equally increase vibrationally or you will be separated in future lives." With a slightly troubled frown, she asked anxiously, "Is this your understanding of how it works, Dick?"

"It makes sense to me, Marcie. And when I read it, I got goose bumps. Tara and I feel that we are counterpart soulmates and we'd like to be together next time, too."

The McGyvers got up to leave. "I'd like to write your case history," I said.

Marcie smiled her approval and Robert added, "That's fine by me but don't use my real last name. I've got to have a little while longer to get used to all of this."

CHAPTER

5

B. J. and Gloria Thomas' Karmic Bond

Gloria Jean Richardson was fourteen when she first heard B. J. Thomas sing on the radio. The song "Mama" filled the room and she shivered as confused thoughts and feelings assailed her.

"Gloria, will you help me to . . ."

"Sh-h-h-h-h!" Gloria snapped at her friend, Marie.

"Oh, come on, Gloria, that's awful. You never listen to anything but hard rock and roll."

"Sh-h-h-h, Marie . . . I mean it!"

As the last strains of the song faded into a commercial, Gloria stood motionless in the middle of the room. "I don't believe how he sings," she said, a tinge of wonder in her voice.

"What are you talking about? You can't stand that kind of music," Marie said, her expression mocking.

"It was his voice. It wasn't the song, and it sure wasn't because I feel anything for my mother," Gloria said, her voice low and far away. "The last time I saw mama was four years ago when she beat the hell out of me one last time before leaving for good."

Gloria turned eighteen during three weeks spent in Houston Memorial Hospital following an auto accident. "A cracked jawbone, missing teeth, a broken kneecap and four hundred facial stitches is a pretty high price to pay for a ride with your boyfriend," said the nurse, as she checked Gloria's pulse.

"He wasn't even my boyfriend," Gloria replied softly. "He was just a friend who needed someone to talk to."

"Who are you going to stay with when you're released?" the nurse asked. "It's going to take you a while to get back on your feet."

"I've written every family member I can think of, telling them I have no money and no place to go. I'm sure one of them will help out." Gloria's tear-smothered voice whispered from behind the bandages covering her entire head and neck.

"Jeeze . . . you look like the mummy herself!" Pam exclaimed. "They wouldn't let me in to see you until today. I don't believe it. I don't believe this could happen, just when you were finally starting to make it on your own." Pam's voice was compassionate but couldn't hide the shock of seeing her best friend in such bad condition.

Gloria attempted to hold back the tears. "I don't have any money to pay for my half of the apartment rent, Pam."

"I know. Yesterday I told the landlord we'd be moving out. I can move back in with my folks, but what will you do?" Pam was apologetic.

"I don't know. I'd rather sleep in the park than move back in with my father and be his punching bag again," Gloria replied unsteadily. Through the bandages, her eyes narrowed. "I'm going to make it. I'm going to make it."

In the sterile hospital room, Gloria faced her fears and assessed her future. The facial injury was her primary concern. She was beautiful. Although not tall enough for high fashion photography, she had become successful modeling for Houston department stores and newspaper ads. Her independence was based upon her appearance, which was now in question.

The pleas for family assistance went unanswered and Gloria left the hospital knowing she was on her own. The doctors gave her a bottle of aspirin and prescriptions for antibiotics and pain medication. The prescriptions were never filled because she simply didn't have the money. Her friends offered moral support, and Kimberly, a high school girlfriend, let Gloria stay in her apartment.

Six weeks after the accident the final facial bandages were removed. "I'm a mess," Gloria said to three of her girlfriends, who were assembled at the apartment for her "coming out" party. "If the scars aren't bad enough, I'll be limping for months and I still have teeth to be dug out." The tensing of her jaw betrayed her deep frustration.

"You look great and we're going to get you back out into the world," Kimberly said. "Tonight, we're all going to Van's Ballroom."

"Only if I can sit in the darkest corner," Gloria replied. She managed a small, tentative smile.

The Van's Ballroom marquee read "B. J. THOMAS" in huge black letters. As Gloria and her friends entered the crowded hall, she recalled her previous reactions to B. J.'s voice. Perplexing emotions surged through her mind as she followed her friends through the maze of people to a table in a dark area close to the stage. The house band was playing at earsplitting volume.

"Ladies and gentlemen, will you please give a warm welcome to B. J. Thomas." The announcer's voice crackled through the din of the crowd. There was a momentary hush followed by boisterous applause. The man in the spotlight was tall and skinny, with curly brown hair. He scanned the room, smiled, nodded, and began to sing "Eyes of a New York Woman."

"God, he looked right at me," Gloria thought, embarrassed and confused by the intensity of her emotions. She crossed her arms and attempted to avoid his gaze. "This is ridiculous, he can't see me in the dark." Kimberly raised her eyebrows, licked her lips and squeezed Gloria's arm. Gloria smiled in response, masking her inner turmoil with deceptive calmness.

Later that night, in bed at Kimberly's apartment, she thought about her reactions. "It was my first night out in so long. I'm nervous about how I look. But I don't look bad. Thank God the scars won't match my fears."

The following morning thoughts of B. J. Thomas were lost in Gloria's concern for making a living. "I can clean and cook," she told Kimberly. "And until I can get back out and hold down a job, I can fix the girls' hair. Before the accident, *Key* magazine was paying me a little to write fillers. I can still do that."

"Let's go back to Van's tonight, before going to the Appleton party," Kimberly said enthusiastically, a week later.

"Will B. J. be on stage?" Gloria asked.

"No, it's somebody else. I don't remember who."

Gloria and Kimberly crossed the dance floor and were about to sit down at a table when a man on her left said, "What are you doing here?" She squinted at his silhouette, her eyes not yet accustomed to the dim light.

"B. J. Thomas?" Gloria asked, hesitatingly. "I didn't think you were singing tonight."

"I'm not, I'm just here with friends," he replied. "I thought you were my sister."

"Do I look like your sister?" Gloria asked, a note of sarcasm in her voice.

"Not really," B. J. replied, coming closer. "Same height and hair color, that's all. But you just seemed so familiar."

"That's a good line."

"No, I mean it," he laughed. "Want to go to the Appleton party with me?"

"I'm already going, so I'll just see you there," Gloria said, feeling her old confidence returning.

"Why not go with me?" B. J. prodded.

"If you're looking for a show horse, you'd better find another stable," she teased before turning serious. "I just went through a windshield, my teeth are knocked out and I'm not ready for this."

The group left Van's together. Outside, B. J. walked up to Gloria, took her arm and guided her under the streetlight. "I really couldn't see what you looked like in there. You're beautiful!"

"Thank you," Gloria responded. "I'll see you at the party." Her voice was shakier than she would have liked.

The party was large and crowded. It was over an hour before she saw B. J. again. "Two different guys have told me they are here with you," he said, more a question than a statement. "When you get your story straight, why don't you come and tell me."

"I can't help what somebody else says. I came by myself and I'm leaving by myself," Gloria replied, boldly meeting his eyes. And she left.

An hour and a half later B. J. was knocking on the apartment door. "It took me this long to find you," he said. The underlying sensuality in his voice captivated her, and she couldn't keep from smiling.

"Good evening, Mr. Thomas, nice to see you again."

It was November 1967—the beginning of a relationship roller coaster ride. December 9, 1968, B. J. and Gloria were married in Las Vegas, Nevada, as "Hooked on a Feeling" was on its way to becoming his second million-selling record. Thirteen months later their daughter Paige was born. "Raindrops Keep Falling on My Head" was topping the charts and the pressure was on.

The faster the money came in the faster they spent it. As success multiplied, so did B. J.'s drug intake. After his performances he would disappear. They decided life in Manhattan was to blame for the wrecked cars, fights, and accelerating drug abuse. So they purchased a beautiful stone country house in Connecticut on four and a half acres of landscaped lawn with a fifty-foot pool.

B. J.'s drug escapades intensified until he finally admitted, "I guess New York wasn't our problem, was it?"

"Oh, B. J., there has to be a way not to hurt so much," Gloria cried. "You've got to get some help. If not for yourself, for Paige and me."

Gloria set up an appointment with a psychiatrist. B. J. saw him for a year with no signs of improvement. When Gloria challenged the doctor, he explained, "If B. J. can accept his anxieties as being normal for him, he can adjust better to the world around him." He handed Gloria a prescription for tranquilizers as she left the office.

Instead of adjusting, B. J. got worse. His "star-struck" psychiatrist was always there to bail him out of jail and rationalize his failures.

"Why don't you leave him?" Gloria's friends asked.

"I couldn't," she would cry. "We both have the same emotionally deprived backgrounds. We need to be loved by each other.

"As long as B. J. has a problem, I have an obligation. It's my problem too," Gloria told her friends. "We'll find a way. We'll get help."

For six years, the Thomases vacillated between being drunk with love and inflicting hate upon each other. The problems with drugs and money continued to escalate until 1974 when Gloria packed enough clothes for Paige and herself, and moved to Fort Worth, Texas.

In the eight months that followed, Gloria and B. J. missed each other so much they forgot their pain and reconciled. The Connecticut house was sold and Nashville became home, but nothing was solved by the separation—the following year was more difficult than any before.

"Just take care of B. J., Gloria," the staff and promoters would plead. "He's got to perform. You've got to make him."

"He can't perform. He's close to killing himself with the drugs!" Gloria would cry.

"You need the money. If he doesn't perform they'll sue, and we can't take another lawsuit," they would counter. "No matter how sick or crazy he is, he can still sing."

In April 1975, B. J.'s recording of "Hey, Won't You Play Another Somebody Done Somebody Wrong Song?" scaled the charts to become another million-seller as Gloria sank into depression. Dazed and hardly functioning, she left again, returning to a rented house in Fort Worth. "I swear I'll never go back to that drug-crazed world again," she cried, over and over. B. J. left Nashville soon after and leased a home in Los Angeles.

Barely able to function, existing in a trancelike stupor, Gloria found a woman to take care of Paige, wash clothes, and cook the meals. Fainting spells followed the depression and culminated with Gloria awakening in the hospital unable to remember what happened. "I can't pay you for eight days in here," she told the doctor. "My husband may be B. J. Thomas but he isn't sending me any money."

"If you'll turn your life over to Jesus Christ, Gloria, everything will work out," said the stranger who befriended her. With the support of her only Fort Worth friends—born-again Christians dedicated to her conversion—Gloria began to pull out of the depression. She found herself once more worrying constantly about B. J.—especially when it was more than a week between phone calls.

"Something has to happen soon," she said to her friends.

"Our entire church is praying for you and B. J.," they would reply.

"God, please—please help me," Gloria sobbed, alone in her bedroom and unable to sleep. As she prayed, the torment eased and faded until a spirit of peace filled her to overflowing. "I give myself to you, God. Without reservation, I surrender everything . . . Paige, B. J., our marriage, my future."

"I'm different, B. J.," she explained on the phone. "I really can't explain what happened to me, but I feel like a new person. It's as if the whole world was lifted from my shoulders."

"You sound different," B. J. replied.

B. J. admitted to a premonition that time was running out for him. He knew he couldn't take drugs forever and sensed he was approaching a final crossroads in his life. "I just don't have any will to live," he said. "I take it one day at a time, not caring if I survive or not."

"Will you come to Fort Worth to visit?" Gloria pleaded. "Paige prayed to God to bring her daddy back to her."

January 1976—B. J. arrived at the Dallas/Fort Worth airport. He was emaciated, carrying only 130 pounds on his six-foot frame. Their initial nervousness with each other soon passed. Although both were wary and careful in their responses, the old love surfaced again in the days that followed. They both felt it. Gloria was a living example of her faith and before the month was out, B. J. also gave his life to God.

It was the end of drugs and the beginning of a new life in Texas. But it was not the end of their problems. Instead of personal conflicts, B. J. and Gloria now focused their attention on B. J.'s career. Irresponsible management had to be replaced and many bad contracts needed to be resolved. Gloria accepted responsibility for this part of the business, freeing B. J. to concentrate upon performing and recording.

B. J.'s acceptance of Christianity opened new doors and his inspirational albums sold well. The concerts now included a mixture of secular and spiritual songs. Although it wasn't a problem for the majority of his fans, many of the born-again Christians would loudly protest and walk out of the auditoriums when he sang "Raindrops Keep Falling on My Head" or any of his other popular songs.

"The Born Agains won't accept me without a cross-examination," he complained to Gloria. "Sometimes I'll say, 'I know I'm a Christian and so does God, whether you or anyone else believes it.' Then they accuse me of hostility."

He received volumes of hateful mail from Born Agains condemning him for charging money to attend his concerts . . . for singing secular songs . . . for not projecting a more loving look on his album covers. "We don't get critical letters from non-Christians," Gloria pointed out. "The poison-pen letters all come from church people."

If the fans were a problem, it was small compared to the Christian promoters. They signed concert contracts and then would not pay, claiming they didn't have the money. B. J. learned early to insist on being paid in advance.

"But isn't this your ministry?" said one promoter.

"No, this is a business," B. J. answered. "I didn't leave my family behind, travel halfway across the United States, pay for my band and people to come with me, so that I could have church with you. I need the money our contract calls for before I go out on that stage."

"You don't have much of a relationship with the Lord to walk out on a concert."

"You must not have much of one either, because you want to cheat me," B. J. snapped in response. "You're charging the people in that auditorium to attend and you even charged them ten dollars to park their cars."

B. J. held his ground, and in all but three instances, the promoters came up with the money they claimed did not exist.

"Since the day I accepted God in my life, I have never doubted the relationship we share," B. J. explained to Gloria. "But I can't accept limited, judgmental attitudes."

"I agree," Gloria replied softly. "Let's just live our lives, our way."

B. J. wanted another baby. Gloria was fearful of

pregnancy. While in Taiwan for a concert, Gloria was introduced to a twelve-day-old Korean baby girl—an orphan in need of a family.

"Are you crazy?" B. J. responded when Gloria proposed adoption.

"Well, you've been saying you want another child. I didn't think it would matter where it came from. It's up to you, B. J."

For weeks they talked about it. "Can we give a child like that the stability she needs?" B. J. asked.

"I don't know," Gloria answered honestly. "All we can do is try."

"We still fight a lot," he mused.

"And we're getting better all the time," Gloria countered.

Soo-me Park was renamed Nora. And from the day she arrived in Texas, she enriched the lives of B. J., Gloria, and nine-year-old Paige. Two weeks after Nora's arrival, Gloria found out she was pregnant. On June 4, 1979, Erin Micah Thomas was born by the Lamaze method. B. J. stayed with his wife, coaching her through the delivery.

Although far from living a life of harmony, the Thomases began to work together on one problem at a time. Two children in diapers limited Gloria's availability for much needed business involvement. Years of bad management resulted in disastrous judgments from the Internal Revenue Service. B. J. and Gloria had identity problems, acceptance problems, and organization problems . . . but month after month, year after year, they remained together through the ups and downs. Slowly, life got better. B. J. won five Grammy awards between 1976 and 1983. Gloria began to write songs—good songs which B. J. and other artists recorded.

The Thomases credited part of the improvement to

an ever-expanding philosophical awareness. Their personal experiences with the born-again Christians demonstrated the limitations of that faith. It had served them well as a transitional phase, but offered little potential for growth. In his twenties, B. J. had studied Edgar Cayce and Paramahansa Yogananda. Reincarnation is the basis of these philosophies, and B. J. and Gloria began to see how metaphysics correlated with the writings of the Bible. Gloria began studying cause and effect, and responded to the justice and logic of karma as a philosophical basis of physical reality.

Since we live in Malibu, California, my wife Tara and I have our share of celebrity friends. But over the years, I've been generally unresponsive to requests from famous people for meetings to discuss reincarnation, or for private past-life regressions. I usually have my staff reply, suggesting a past-life regressionist I feel will do a good job, and we offer them a pass to a forthcoming seminar. If they attend, we provide a false name tag to disguise their participation, but for those with famous faces this seldom works. I can understand celebrities' reluctance to expose themselves to public gatherings.

During two periods of my life, I have worked as a past-life therapist, counseling individuals. But today, unless onstage communicating to a seminar audience, I prefer a reclusive existence of working with my own publishing company staff on tapes and communications projects. Or, even better, to sit at home in front of my word processor, writing books or magazine articles about metaphysics and New Age philosophy.

June 1984: "B. J. Thomas' staff contacted the office," I explained to Tara over dinner. "He and his wife are going to be in town and would like to meet with me." My wife was once a Hollywood model who later worked for Warner Brothers and Columbia movie studios. She often turned down acting opportunities in favor of her position in studio security. The studio experiences left her generally unimpressed by celebrities.

Tara thought for a long moment. "I think you should see them," she said.

"Why?" I listed the names of famous people we'd turned down. "Why B. J. Thomas?"

"I don't know. It's just a feeling. Besides, you like his music," Tara said.

My office cleared the meeting with the Thomas office in Arlington, Texas, and gave them our unlisted home phone number. A few days later the phone rang, "Richard, this is B. J. Thomas . . ."

As much as I dislike communicating with strangers over the phone, B. J. was one of the easiest people I had ever talked to. There was an instant affinity—like talking to a long-lost friend. He later admitted that he shared my aversion to phone conversations as well as the sense of easy familiarity during that first call.

The Thomases arrived in their touring bus after driving all night following a concert. The six members of the band were still asleep in the hotel when Tara and I picked up Gloria and B. J. after lunch. The sense of familiarity was even stronger in person, and the four of us shared an afternoon of enjoyable conversation about many things, including reincarnation.

Neither B. J. nor Gloria had experienced past-life regression, so I explained the hypnotic process, set up recording equipment and for two hours guided first B. J., then Gloria through several shared past lifetimes. The past incarnations offered some cause and effect explanations relating to their present relationship and Higher-Self advice for the future. Long after dark we drove them back to the hotel where the staff and band were preparing the bus for the road.

Since our initial meeting, we have vacationed together as families with all our kids on the tour bus. Gloria uses our spare bedroom as a West Coast hideaway when in Los Angeles, working on songwriting projects. Tara and Gloria stay in regular contact by phone, and in February 1987, B. J. called to say he would be in town to appear on the "Hour Magazine" TV show. We arranged to have dinner at the Hollywood Roosevelt Hotel after the show taping.

"I'm writing a new book about predestined love for Simon & Schuster. Are you willing to be in it, B. J.?" I asked during the meal.

"Sure, man," he replied without hesitation. "Since Gloria and I combined metaphysical awareness with our faith, life works better than ever. It even helped me recently stop smoking. But I picked up twenty pounds right here." He patted his stomach. "Check with Gloria, she's been working with a local psychic and has some interesting new information."

B. J.'s Past-Life Regressions: The first impressions B. J. received were of himself as a young boy in Switzerland in 1742. He was walking with his grandmother to their cottage. (It was later discovered that Gloria was his grandmother in that life. "I loved him, I pampered him, I was very sweet to him . . . I took care of him," she explained in a cross-verification regression.)

When projected forward in time, he perceived images of being a bank accountant who was very worried about money. "I mishandled the money," he said sadly. Further questioning uncovered his use of drugs. Then a room with no doors or windows formed into a bank vault, and as he drew back from the cramped environment, he saw himself lying on the floor with a gun in his hand.

From a Higher-Self level of awareness, B. J. explained that his money problems in this life are a direct carry-over from his mishandling of money in the Swiss incarnation.

The next lifetime we explored was in France. B. J. saw himself with long hair, dressed in beautiful clothes. His name was Cerril and his wife (Gloria) was Antoinette. The marriage was good, but he described the lifetime as "frivolous." As an aristocrat, he commanded a great deal of power. When instructed to move forward to an important event, he saw himself older, with white hair. "I've just won a horse race," he said proudly. "Everyone is looking at me. But, of course, they have to."

In a third life exploration, B. J. was an opera singer in the 1800s. His voice was widely acclaimed and he described himself as being "grand." Further questions and answers disclosed that he always had plenty of money and was waited on hand and foot. "I didn't know how to love myself," he explained from Higher Self. "I was terribly fat—blowing myself out of proportion."

"What is the primary lesson to be learned from the lifetime?" I asked.

"To learn the importance of giving of myself," was his immediate reply.

Finding no connection to Gloria in this regression, I called her in May 1987. "Were you involved in B. J.'s life as an opera singer?" I asked.

"He didn't say anything about it in his regression, but it's strange that you should ask that now, Richard. Shirley J. Smith—a psychic here in Arlington—recently said to me, 'Did you know you worked in the music business with B. J. a long time ago? You used to write opera.' "

"And Shirley knew nothing of the regression?" I questioned.

"Nothing!"

Gloria's Past-Life Regressions: Gloria's first impressions were of a young girl named Rebecca riding in the back of a covered wagon. She was tending her sick and pregnant mother, and described an older boy (B. J.) who was outside pulling the cattle. While her father was away from the wagon, hunting, Rebecca helped her mother give birth to a baby boy who quickly died. By the time her father returned, her mother was also dead.

When projected forward to an important time in the future, Rebecca was twenty-six and giving birth to her first child. She had married the boy accompanying the wagon, and did not want to be pregnant. "I was so afraid of pregnancy I refused to have sex with him for years," she explained. "It was the only way I knew not to get pregnant." The birth of their daughter went well. "But after that I just turned my head and lived the social image of a wife," Gloria explained after the regression. "It was our agreement that he resolve his sexual needs somewhere else. We lived in a small town, and B. J. took care of everything. I didn't have to worry about anything but the house. After crossing over into spirit, as an old woman, I realized it was a very timid life. I was a sweet person but I hid from things. B. J. died three days after me in that incarnation."

In a second regression, Gloria found herself in an ancient Greek lifetime. "I have blond hair and blue eyes, and my name is Colire," she explained in a sweet voice. B. J. maintained an important position in the society. "I serve, honor, and worship him," she said, before proudly stating, "And I've given him fourteen fine children."

During our May 1987 phone conversation, I asked Gloria if Shirley J. Smith had uncovered any information that might provide additional understanding.

"She has told me of a lifetime B. J. and I shared in Egypt. He was an entertainer in the palace. I was a beautiful woman and of a higher social position. We were secret lovers, but I was very flamboyant and just toyed with people's lives. The scars I carry on my face today are a karmic balance relating directly back to that lifetime.

"Shirley says I returned with B. J. in this life to learn to be responsible and to deal with some hard issues. B. J. and I are here to learn to harmonize and attain a vibrational attunement we've set as a spiritual goal. Plus, we're paying back a lot of karma. Karmically we arranged it so there is no way to run away from ourselves or each other. You know our background, Richard. As hard as we've both tried, it's been impossible for B. J. and I to get rid of each other. There have been times when neither of us wanted to be around the other, yet neither could leave. And if we did it was never for long. Did you know I was once in extensive therapy for co-dependency because I thought I was crazy? I thought, 'I'm a very sick person acting out her life.'

"But when you asked for copies of the past-life regression tapes, I listened to them again and realized how much progress we've made in three years. We've been working on the things we most need to learn. And as we learn, life gets better."

"Wisdom erases karma," I said lightly.

"Both B. J. and I will buy that." She laughed.

CHAPTER

6

Susie Madden and the Marine

Susie looked up from straightening the sweater display to see Robert, the pride of Salt Lake City's U.S. Marine recruiters, standing militantly before her with another marine. "Susie, this is Don, he's my replacement. Don, Susie is assistant manager of this wonderful boutique."

"Hi, Robert," Susie replied. "Is your next assignment going to be more exciting than recruiting high school kids in a shopping mall? Hi, Don." She held out her hand and looked into his eyes as he stared at her. She felt a flicker of recognition, and she bit her lip as she resisted a panicked reaction. He was looking into her very soul.

"Oh, my God, I know you—I know you completely," she thought wildly as an electrifying shudder reverberated through her. "I've loved you before." Her thoughts whirled out of control for what seemed like minutes.

"I'm very glad to meet you," Don said, cupping his other hand over hers and squeezing it lightly.

Moments later, Robert was escorting Don into the next store in the Cottonwood Mall to complete his rounds of introductions. Delma, the store manager, looked at Susie. "Are you all right?"

"Yes, yes. It's just that I thought I recognized Don for a moment, but it was silly."

"Well, he certainly noticed you. You could drown in those big brown eyes of his, couldn't you?" Delma laughed. "Anyway, it will be a lot nicer to have Don working upstairs. Robert always bugged me."

"Me, too," Susie replied vaguely, her mind going over her reaction to the tall marine. "How foolish. How could I think I know a man I just met? I certainly have never met him in this life! That leaves only reincarnation, and I don't know that much about past lives."

Susie experienced the same reaction when she ran into Don at the fast-food stand where she went for morning coffee, and again the following Friday in the crowded mall restaurant when they shared a table. She attempted to explain it to Delma. "There is such an intense familiarity, excitement, and sense of anticipation, it makes me crazy. I really feel like I know the inner man completely. It is only the surface aspects that are new to me, and it's delightful getting to know them."

"Sounds like love to me," Delma responded as she hung the latest shipment of designer pants on the circular rack. "Love makes everybody crazy and explains everything."

Susie straightened the earring display, glad no customers were in the store. "It's very strange, Delma. I sense he is afraid of me while at the same time he is drawn to me, in spite of his resistance."

"Nothing unusual about a male being afraid of a relationship which might lead to commitment," Delma said. "Look at you. You're the prettiest nineteen-year-old in town. Has he asked you out yet?"

"This Saturday night," she said softly, her eyes gazing blindly at the display.

Monday morning Susie reported, "The evening was wonderful!" And so was the next evening and the next and the next they spent together.

"Then why do I sense that it isn't going exactly the way you'd write the script?" Delma asked.

"I just love being with him," Susie said, smiling secretly as she spoke. "I haven't told him, but I love him. I know how much he likes to be with me, but he keeps his distance, hardly ever touching me. I sense these intense underlying currents of desire and fear within him. Last night we were watching TV at his house, and he just took a deep breath and plunged into his feelings. It was as though he suddenly surrendered—there was a feeling of desperation about it."

"How was it?" Delma asked, in a low, sexy voice.

"Delma! Well, it was very intense and passionate."

Susie and Don now centered their lives around each other, quickly becoming very close and sharing more and more of themselves. She was blond, 5'11", thin-hipped and slender. Don was 6'2", a dark, powerful figure of a man. "We complement each other quite well," she would say, putting a hand on his shoulder and suggestively rolling her hips.

Their weeks together became months of a mutually enjoyed routine—driving together each morning to the mall, located in Holladay, a suburb of Salt Lake City. Lunches were usually picnics eaten in a nearby park, until the fall weather forced them indoors to discover a hideaway basement restaurant they nicknamed "The Den of Iniquity."

The first snow of the season was falling one morning when Susie arrived at work, her eyes red and swollen. "Good Lord, child, it looks like you cried all night. What happened?"

"I don't even know, Delma. Just as I've come to feel safe and comfortable, sure of both our feelings, Don has drawn away from me. He's given no explanations, he's just become distant, silent, and impenetrable. We won't be seeing each other for a while." She sobbed, futilely attempting to shield her face from Delma's gaze.

Four months later, Don reentered Susie's life, again plunging headlong into an all-consuming love affair. A call to overseas duty followed. He wrote daily letters from Hong Kong, the Philippines, Guam, and Hawaii. Upon his return, they again lived together and their love grew even more intense. Susie was again feeling safe and secure in the relationship when Don withdrew into silence for two months.

Then, as if nothing had happened, he was back—stronger, closer, more desperate than before. "I'm so afraid I'll let you down," he said to Susie. "I know I'll let you down and you won't love me anymore. You'll leave, I know you'll leave. I'm just a loser . . . a failure."

"Don, those terms don't fit you. I know you—you're a winner. Now stop it. You won't let me down, and I won't leave you. I love you. Don't you have any idea how very, very much I love you?"

He smiled lovingly at her and shook his head. "Let's make it work, honey. I love you, too."

The months of bliss lasted until shortly after Don received word of his transfer to Santa Ana. Susie resigned her job and was packing for the move they would make together when Don disappeared once more into his cold, silent world. Susie cried and pleaded. She held him in the darkness and whispered loving words in his ear as she ran her hands through his hair for hours. His only response was a hostile glare.

On the morning of the day they were scheduled to move, her body was engulfed in weariness. She felt drained, hollow, lifeless. "I can't keep going through this, Don. You're going to have to go to California alone," she said, standing in the middle of a room piled high with taped cardboard cartons. He responded by moving the boxes containing his belongings to the other side of the room. By late afternoon Don's boxes were gone and Susie was alone in the apartment they no longer leased.

"Oh, my God," she cried. "Universe, or my guides, or whoever is out there, please help me to understand why I feel such a strong connection with him. Why do I feel compelled to always be there when he wants me? Why do I have such a strong need to reassure him? Why is he so afraid of a relationship with me? *I need some answers! Please . . . please . . . please!*"

Susie fell on the bed, crying. There was a brief moment of dizziness and resistance as she let go of her painful physical world and spontaneously began to see mental images. She would later describe the experience as "two hours of exquisitely sharp and clear visualizations, voices, and feelings so real and so intense I didn't know if I was remembering them, or living them. I was seeing through her eyes and experiencing every intimate feeling. At one point I sat up screaming, wanting the impressions to stop, but they continued until it was over."

The following is Susie's exact description of her experience: "One minute I was lying on my bed crying and the next I was in Poland just prior to World War II. I was young, probably fourteen or fifteen, and very infatuated with a young boy in our neighborhood. He was a year or two older than I, and exceptionally bright in school. In my mind's eye, I can still see the street we lived on, and feel the sunshine. I felt an optimistic hope. We had everything to look forward to.

"My next image was of hiding. My family and I were in a cramped, dark room with only one small, grimy window. I felt we had been hiding there for nearly two years. Then a friend of the family came to the door asking for me. Taking my hand, she led me down a long, narrow hallway. I kept asking where we were going, but she only laughed and told me to hurry. At last we reached a doorway at the end of the hall. She opened the door and stepped back, smiling. I walked, dazed, into the room filled with light and air—and the boy I had loved, now grown into manhood. I even saw the specks of dust in the air, dancing in the sunlight streaming through an open window. I felt his arms around me and I experienced his lovemaking for the first time that night.

"He was in the Polish resistance. My family was Jewish. For different reasons, we were both hiding from the Nazis. After being secretly married, we moved into an apartment of our own. I remember sitting in the dark with the curtains drawn. I was nursing a newborn daughter and torn by mixed emotions. Our family life was happy, but it was also filled with fear due to his resistance work. Each time he left home, I didn't know if he would come back again. And I knew that by marrying a Jewess, he put himself in even more danger. I held my child closely and prayed for a miracle that would allow us to survive this madness. I had remained safely hidden for over three years. Perhaps, with God's help, it would continue.

"The visualizations then blurred, and I began to perceive German soldiers roughly pushing us down a long, twisting staircase. I was clutching my child, now about six months old, trying not to fall on the stairs. I remember being mesmerized by the rifle held by a soldier at the foot of the flight of stairs. When we reached him, he put the butt of the rifle into my back and pushed me on down the next flight. Many emotions were racing through me: terror, shock, surprise, and some hope. We had heard terrible rumors about what they were doing to Jews, but we couldn't believe them. Surely, no one could treat other human beings in that way. It couldn't possibly be true.

"The horror of hiding was over. What was to come had to be better. We reached the street and I saw a truck backed up near the door of the apartment house. People were being shoved into the back of this truck, and I could see them huddling on benches along the side of the interior. My child was crying. I tried to comfort her, but she continued to cry. Suddenly, a soldier tore my daughter out of my arms, threw her to the ground, and stabbed her through the chest with his bayonet while I helplessly watched.

"I began screaming. I heard rough voices but could not understand them. I felt my husband's arms around me and heard him tell me I must be quiet. I heard the soldiers tell him that he did not have to go to the ghetto with me. He was not Jewish, he had only made the mistake of living with a Jewess, and he was free to stay where he was. He tightened his grip on me and told them that he would go with me. I can still see the proud tilt of his head as he spoke these words. We were then pushed into the truck. My husband sat beside me on the bench along the left side of the truck. Tears streamed down my cheeks, and I felt myself beginning to withdraw, turning inward, going numb and silent . . . consumed by the images of my daughter's murder.

"We were transported directly to the Warsaw ghetto which had earlier been the Jewish section of town. The Germans had walled it in and were bringing in Jews from all over Poland to live there, the final step before the death camps.

"What followed was a long, dark time during which I saw and felt almost nothing. I knew where we were and that every day hundreds of people were taken away in trucks. I knew that my husband was involved with a group of people in the ghetto who wanted to fight the Germans rather than continue dying in silence. We could no longer doubt the rumors of the death camps and the atrocities, and it had incensed some people enough to begin fighting back. They knew there was no hope—they wanted to die proudly, fighting, rather than be silently murdered.

"I was unable to respond to these things; I withdrew even from my husband. My days were spent staring out the window of our apartment which was on one of the top floors of the building. Although I had enough awareness to feel guilty about withdrawing from my husband, I couldn't seem to help myself. I remained alive only through the loving care of my husband and his friends' wives. As much as I wanted to live again and let him know of my love, I couldn't break through the numbness engulfing me.

"Our apartment building, once crammed to overflowing with people, was now nearly empty. The streets were empty, except for sporadic battles when the Germans tried to enter. My husband and his friends attempted to get me to move to a room underground where it would be safer, but I insisted on staying where I could see out my window. The thought of being locked up again in a dark room was more than I could bear. I remained by my window and watched as flames leaped high into the night sky, while the Germans bombed the ghetto in an attempt to quell the Jewish resistance.

"Suddenly, one morning my numbness broke. Hate and rage flooded my awareness. Down on the street, I could see the German soldiers marching, guns at ready, warily eyeing the windows and doorways along their route. I started running. I heard my husband yell at me to stop. As I ran down the flights of stairs, I could hear his footsteps following frantically behind me. Reaching the bottom of the stairway, I burst out the door of the building and ran toward a young German soldier in the center of the street. Although I had no weapon, I was determined to kill him, knowing it would mean my life. My rage and despair were so great that I wanted to kill just one of them in payment for my daughter and my family and friends. As I ran toward him I was confronted by startled, icy blue eyes filled with disgust. It was as if he were looking at the most loathsome vermin on earth. In that split second, I realized the enormity of their hatred for us—a hatred strong enough to generate the madness we had been living for years. He was young—sixteen or seventeen at most. I realized he had been raised with that hatred and knew nothing else. Strangely enough, I understood him as he raised his rifle and fired.

"The bullet struck me in the chest and I fell to the ground, still looking up at him. My husband ran up to me and kneeled, taking me into his arms. I heard the soldier order him to leave me. He ignored the command and continued to cradle me. I watched as a bullet from the soldier's gun blew away the back of my husband's head and I felt him slump against me as everything went black."

Sunday morning, Delma dropped by Susie's apartment. "I couldn't believe it when you called," Delma said over coffee, sitting at Susie's kitchen table. "I thought you were long gone."

Susie nodded. "Me, too. You're my friend, Delma.

You've been my only confidante during this entire misadventure with Don. You've been there since the first meeting, remember?"

Susie related the spontaneous regressive experience, although she knew Delma didn't accept the concept of reincarnation. "When it was over I stayed up all night, pacing, crying, and reviewing what I had experienced. I knew my husband in that life was Don in this life, and he died only because he loved me so much. He chose to enter the ghetto with me because of that love. How could he help but have a subconscious fear that loving me might mean disastrous consequences. My withdrawal and mental illness following the death of my child caused him to feel abandoned. In this life, Don has a terrible fear of abandonment. I think I understand why he mentally leaves me before I can abandon him, and why he is torn between his desires and his fears."

"Susie, Susie . . . this is incredible. Do you really accept all this?" Delma asked, holding her coffee cup with both hands almost as a shield of protection. "If this is true, then everyone else would also have relationships based upon past lives. Even Ralph and I, heaven forbid. Once around the block with him is all I want to experience."

Susie laughed at Delma's reaction. "It certainly feels true, Delma. Karma is logical and it explains all the inequality in the world. It also explains why Don was so fearful of letting me down . . . of not being good enough, and why he felt like a loser and a failure. He fought so desperately in the resistance and in the ghetto, without succeeding. In the end, he was unable to save my life or the life of our child. It's this inner awareness he hasn't come to terms with."

"How can you come to terms with something you

aren't consciously aware of?" Delma asked, shaking her head at the lack of logic.

"If karma is the basis of physical reality, then we are here to learn to let go of fear. When I say that, I mean all the fear-based emotions: anger, selfishness, jealousy, hate, repression, greed, possessiveness, envy, guilt, and all the rest. It is these fears that have trapped us on the wheel of reincarnation. Once we resolve them, we'll be free. It doesn't matter if you are aware of the fears—you're here to work through them at your own pace."

"What about *your* fears in regard to the situation?" Delma asked.

"I don't think I've come to terms with my withdrawal and the way I abandoned him in Poland. Just thinking about it now, I feel guilty for allowing him to enter the ghetto with me," Susie replied. Her tone was apologetic.

"That's ridiculous," Delma snapped. "You were in shock. Your baby had just been murdered. You couldn't have been thinking of such things and he couldn't have left you without creating some bad karma. Oh, my God. I'm talking like I accept all this."

They both laughed together and moved to the couch in the living room. "I'm glad he left you the furniture," Delma said, looking around the room. "But I guess that isn't something you need to play marine."

"That's another interesting thing, Delma. Don died fighting in Poland, and in this life he joined the marines at seventeen and was so gung ho, he did two tours in Vietnam."

"Maybe he wanted to get another shot at the bad guys," Delma said, almost inaudibly. "So what happens next, Susie?"

"1981 is going to be the year we make it work.

Maybe our fourth attempt to establish a solid relationship is what it will take to overcome the fear of the ghetto. I'm going to call him and see if he is willing to give it another try."

"And if he isn't?"

"Then I'll wait three months and try again. I need to reassure him, to build him up, to let him know he is loved. I have to let him know that I believe in him completely."

"Are you going to tell him about your regressive experience?" Delma asked.

"No, I don't think so. Don doesn't accept my metaphysical ideas. He'd think it was a rationale to justify what has happened."

"That's a possibility, isn't it?" Delma said, getting up to leave.

"No, it isn't," Susie replied with cool authority.

Life for Don and Susie in Santa Ana was good again for over a year. But in September of 1982, he moved alone to Hawaii and Susie returned to Salt Lake City. "You'll just become disappointed in me, or I'll become disappointed in you," he said. "I know we would separate eventually, and it would only hurt more later."

Susie claims she was able to release the relationship fully and with love in 1983. "He wasn't willing to face his fears in this life, and I can't judge him for that," she told me. "But I was able to love him, understand him, and release him. I believe I have been able to let go of my fears created in our past. I have forgiven myself for the mistakes I made in the past life and this one, too. In so doing, I released my grief and the need I felt to make something up to Don."

"Was there anything else that helped you to let go?" I asked.

"Yes. I asked for help from my guides. In another spontaneous subjective experience I was allowed to see what our relationship would be like if I failed to let go. As hard as it has been for me to accept, the energies and misunderstandings of our previous incarnation remain. This vision showed a very painful and destructive relationship which would have manifested itself if we were to remain together. It was right after this experience I truly let Don go and released my energy from the past, allowing it the freedom to heal in its own way."

"Since you've been able to experience such powerful regressions on your own, have you ever explored if you've been together with Don in other lifetimes?" I asked.

"Oh yes, we've had two happy, long-term relationships that I know of. I've seen images and full scenarios of a life in the Deep South prior to the Civil War and one in medieval Europe. I'm sure there are others, and I know we'll be together again in a future life."

Following her final separation from Don, Susie focused her energy on fine art. A gallery sponsored a one-man show and she participated in many group exhibits in Utah, Montana, and New Mexico from 1983 to October 1985 when she experienced a block.

"I found myself strangely unable to do any artwork," Susie explained. "I realized I was experiencing some sort of inner transformation. A study of New Age philosophy helped me understand this spiritual awakening. I now work in Salt Lake City as a psychic channel and healer, helping others to resolve their emotional problems and grow spiritually. As a channel, I can relate past-life awareness from their spirit guides. Knowing why you have a problem is the first step to liberation."

CHAPTER

7

Randi Mabrey's Family Ties

The extended family traveled in mobile homes like a small band of gypsies, following the southwestern agricultural jobs. Grandparents, brothers and sisters, aunts, uncles and cousins, they had always lived together on the outskirts of whatever town they were in. Parking in remote areas and never staying long in one place, they depended upon each other for assistance and companionship. Randi was an only child; her closest friend was cousin Becki, three years younger and the only girl in her immediate family of eight children.

In the 1960s the two girls were together in high school. Randi was a husky tomboy with golden brown hair and an outgoing personality. Becki was dark, petite, and rather fragile-looking.

"You're more like a sister than a cousin," Randi said, one day as they walked home from school. Their path led through a dusty field scorched by the 105-degree Arizona heat.

"Yeah, but if I were your sister, we'd fight more than we do," Becki replied. "And you probably wouldn't be my great protector."

"Your great protector?"

"Yes," Becki said, laughing. "You ought to see yourself when we double-date. You're more protective of me than my own father would be."

"Maybe I am," Randi responded. "But if you were to tell your father all the secrets you share with me, you'd be in big trouble."

The cousins remained close over the years that followed although occasionally there were bouts of anger. These were usually experienced by Becki when she felt Randi had let her down or betrayed her in some way.

Becki settled in California and studied hypnotherapy. Randi became a hairstylist; an interest in metaphysical work eventually took her to Sedona, Arizona. In 1980, at the age of thirty, Randi scheduled a session with a hypnotist to explore past lives in general. The following is her description of one incarnation which relates directly to her predestined, sisterly love for Becki:

"When the hypnotist asked my name, I explained that I was George Michael Brown, the son of Anna and Michael Brown of Des Moines, Iowa. As the impressions began to unfold, I knew I was a tall, skinny barber with a girlfriend named Lucy. Lucy was small, dark, and frail. She was dying of leukemia. In my feelings of helplessness, I swore to her, again and again, that she would get well and I would always take care of her.

"After she died, I went into the army. The year was 1943, and I was twenty-two years old. The next impressions were of our ship docking in England; from there we went to Paris for a layover en route to Italy. It was in Paris that I met a lovely lady who swept me off my feet. Soon, we were meeting for passionate afternoon liaisons. During one of our romantic interludes, her husband burst through the doors of the bedroom, carrying a pistol. He fired, and the bullet struck me straight in the heart. Everything went black.

"Before awakening me, the hypnotist asked if I knew anyone from the past lifetime in my current life. In response, the face of my cousin Becki appeared before my inner eyes. Superimposed on it was the face of Lucy."

The experience was so powerful, Randi felt compelled to call Becki in California. "I was a man in my last lifetime," Randi said, "and you were my girlfriend. Your name was . . ."

"Lucy," Becki interrupted, "and I died of leukemia."

Randi gasped disbelievingly. She couldn't respond.

"It's got to be real, Randi," Becki said. "I experienced that lifetime last year while trading hypnotic regressions with another hypnotherapist. I meant to tell you about it, but I guess I forgot. Do you know what else impressed me about the regression?"

"No, what?" Randi replied, beginning to recover from the shock.

"Remember when we were kids? You were seven or eight, and for a year or so everybody in the family tagged you with the nickname of 'George.' "

Randi's case demonstrates how love draws people back together into destined relationships, although not always as lovers. While interviewing Randi about her experience, I said, "If you died in your last life in 1943 or 1944, and were born into your current life in 1950, you certainly weren't on the other side very long, were you?"

"No, not long enough for my etheric body to fully heal," she said, nodding her head in agreement.

"So you were born with a physical problem, weren't you?"

"Yes. I was born with heart disease," she replied. "Because I died from a bullet in the heart and returned so quickly, my heart problems were assured."

Note: Metaphysicians generally agree that the *etheric body* is the matrix that holds the four bodies of man together. It is affected by the nature of the *astral body* and the *mental body,* and ensures that the *physical body* is a reflection of the soul inhabiting the form. The *etheric body* exists between the physical and astral, separating completely at death.

When you have raised your vibrational rate to the level where it is no longer necessary to reincarnate upon the earth, you will exist in your *mental body* in the nonphysical realms of spirit.

CHAPTER

8

Evelyn Koski and the Stranger

"Law offices," Evelyn said automatically into the phone. On the other end of the line was her cousin Larry, whom she had not been in touch with for several years. He had recently reappeared in her life, and they had enjoyed many long conversations of "remember when." They exchanged the usual pleasantries and she asked where he was calling from.

"I'm between planes in Chicago, on my way to Terre Haute. A man I just met on the flight is here, and he wants to speak with you," he replied.

"And you're calling me in Birmingham to tell . . ." She stopped in midsentence, realizing there was no one on the other end. Waiting, she tapped her pen on the pink phone memo pad, expecting a relative or old friend to begin speaking at any moment. To her surprise, the voice was that of a complete stranger—a soft, deep, resonant male voice.

"Hello! My name is Louis Santell, I live in Chicago and I just met your cousin on the plane," he said hesitantly. Suppressing a sigh, Evelyn rolled her eyes to the ceiling of the rosewood paneled office. To her amazement, as she listened to Lou talk about his career in sales and other things unimportant to her, she began to feel a response stirring deep within her. But, despite her legal training, she could not remain focused upon his words, no matter how hard she tried.

"I've really enjoyed talking to you. May I call you tomorrow?" he asked.

"Yes, sure, that would be nice," she replied. "Good-bye." Evelyn replaced the receiver in the telephone cradle, wondering why the call had created such an emotional reaction. It certainly wasn't based on anything that had been said, or what she could remember of it.

"Anything wrong?" Marie asked from across the room. Marie was the firm's second legal secretary, as well as Evelyn's friend and confidante.

Evelyn stared out the window into the garden courtyard. It was raining lightly, and the first leaves of spring were beginning to bloom. "No . . . nothing at all," she replied in a faraway voice.

Thinking about the call, Evelyn decided, "Crazy Larry obviously shared a few drinks with Louis, instigated the call, and that will be the end of that."

"So much for my analytical, left hemisphere-oriented brain," she thought an hour later when Lou called again.

"Evelyn, I don't understand it," he said, attempting to justify the call. "I'm a salesman, I talk to people all day, every day, and I search for excuses to find quiet time. But, for some reason, I just had to talk to you again. I really don't know why."

"Well, I don't want to sound silly, but as you talked to me, something inside of me responded to you, too," she said. She began to ask Lou about his life. "Yes, I'm single. You, too? What are your interests and hobbies?"

Evelyn was still thinking about their conversations when she opened the door to her condo and was greeted by Rupert, her Manx cat. Rupert anxiously awaited the feeding ritual every evening at 6 P.M. and sulked when his mistress remained in town for a dinner date.

"All right, old boy," she said, scooping the cat into her arms. Rupert purred in response as she carried him into the bedroom where he jumped from her arms to the bed and then to the makeup table, where he sat watching while Evelyn changed from her wool business suit to cotton slacks and a casual blouse.

Catching a glimpse of her reflection in the dresser mirror, Evelyn stopped, tilted her head to one side, placed her hands on her hips and spoke directly to herself. "You're pretty damned attractive for a lady in her late thirties. You've got a great job and all the comforts of the good life but your romantic life is going nowhere, Evelyn. You're so vulnerable, you're being turned on by meaningless phone calls from a stranger."

In the days that followed, Evelyn found herself eagerly awaiting Lou's calls—usually several a day. After two months, he announced his plans to come to Birmingham. "I'll fly in late in the afternoon on Friday," he explained. "We can have dinner together, but I'll have to fly back to Chicago later in the evening to be here for a sales meeting Saturday morning."

"I'll be at the airport," Evelyn said, "but we've never even exchanged pictures. How will I recognize you?"

"You have a general idea what I look like," he laughed. "Just be there—I'm sure we'll know each other."

Evelyn arrived at the airport forty minutes early and sat watching the lights of the runway until flight 710 from Chicago was announced over the loudspeaker. "Why am I so nervous?" she thought, as she waited for the passengers to come up the ramp from the plane. "I'm acting like a schoolgirl, yet . . ." Her thoughts froze in midstream when her eyes lit on a middle-aged, slightly balding man and she experienced a shock of instant recognition. His smile went straight to her heart.

"I knew it was you the moment I stepped into the gate area," Lou said, taking her hand. "I don't believe this, I really don't. I know you. We've never met before, but I know you."

Lou was forty-five, slightly overweight, with a bald patch developing at his crown. His dark, affectionate eyes were his outstanding feature. He wore an immaculate, dark-colored business suit, white shirt, and maroon tie. Conversation was even easier in person than on the phone and Lou had Evelyn relaxed and laughing before they left the arrival gate. The date was everything they had hoped to experience, and it served to intensify the telephone conversations. Later that evening she cried as she watched his plane lift off the runway and disappear into the darkness.

Lou began calling from Chicago as many as six or seven times a day. He often flew to Birmingham for weekends, and Evelyn would meet him in Chicago. In the summer, they vacationed together at a secluded lake.

"Aren't you ever going to marry him?" asked Marie, as she glanced over the lunch menu. "For the last two years, the two of you have spent half your lives on the phone and you live for the next time you'll be together. I don't understand."

"I'm not so sure I do, either." Evelyn smiled as she beckoned the waiter to their table. "I swear they have better service at McDonald's," she said softly.

"And you're changing the subject, Evelyn," Marie chided.

"Marie, I've spent a thousand hours attempting to analyze my relationship with Lou. It is totally illogical, but it's the most wonderful thing I've ever experienced. I have such an incredible love for him and yet, with our personality traits and life-styles, I just can't imagine us being married."

"How does he feel?" Marie asked.

"The same way I do. We've talked a great deal about it and we just don't want to spoil what we have."

Marie picked at her salad and shook her head. "I guess I envy you anyway. I've never felt that deeply about anyone."

Evelyn sighed, rolling her necklace between her thumb and index finger. "I don't know if I'm afraid of failure or afraid of success. I don't think I'm paranoid. Sure, I've been hurt by relationships in the past, but no more than anyone else I know."

"If the two of you ever get together, you'll be able to afford matching sports cars just on the money you two would save on phone bills," Marie laughed.

Evelyn agreed and then asked, "Will you cover for me this afternoon between two and four? I've got to go to the doctor about a couple of lumps I found in my breast. And if Lou calls, please try to calm him down. I put off telling him until last night, and he was just absolutely hysterical. Then, just before we left for lunch today, he called to tell me he spent the entire morning in church praying for my health. It was the first time he's been inside a church in over thirty years."

Marie was smiling and holding the phone out to Evelyn when she stepped back into the law offices at 4:05 P.M. "Guess who?" she said teasingly.

"Yes, Lou . . . yes. NO. The X rays revealed lumps of a benign nature, according to the doctor. And I love you, and you're crazy. Okay, but call me after I get home. Marie has been doing my work all afternoon and I've got to help her get caught up before five. Love you, too. Bye."

The two years became four and the relationship continued as before. Evelyn dated other men occasionally, but Lou continued to be the love of her life. Long-distance love, but intense and fulfilling nonetheless.

Then, late one Friday afternoon in February, Lou called from the Denver airport to tell Evelyn he was boarding a plane to Chicago. "I'll call you as soon as I get home, Monkey," he said. Evelyn hung up the phone. As she got up from her desk, she stood momentarily blank and shaken, then fell back into the chair. "What's wrong?" Marie yelled frantically.

"I don't know," Evelyn gasped. She attempted to get up again, but collapsed to the floor. Marie dashed to her side, calling for help.

"No, Marie, no. Wait . . . please," Evelyn pleaded.

"Do you hurt? Where's it hurt?" Marie demanded fearfully.

"Here . . . in the area of my gall bladder. A searing pain, but it's going away. It really is. Would you please get me a drink of water?"

She sipped the water Marie brought her, and sat up. "It's gone, the pain is gone. I'm fine, Marie, don't worry," she said as she stood up, adjusting her skirt. After assuring the law partners of her well-being, Evelyn sat beside Marie on the couch in the empty office waiting room. "Wow, that was incredible. I hurt so bad, but all I could see, almost like a dream, was Lou's face in front of me, distorted with pain."

"You mean, he hurt because you hurt?" Marie asked, placing her hand on Evelyn's forehead as if checking for a fever.

"I guess," Evelyn replied, leaning back on the couch with her eyes shut. "His face was there, vividly at first, then just slowly fading away."

Evelyn waited for the call Lou had promised to make upon his return to Chicago. At midnight, she called him but only reached his answering machine. All weekend, she continued to call as her concern grew into panic.

It was Monday morning, shortly after her arrival at the law offices, that she received a call from a Chicago hospital. "Is this Miss Evelyn Koski? I've agreed to place this call in an attempt to calm down one of our patients."

Then came the barely audible whisper, "Ciucci, I love you." It was Lou! The nurse came back on the line and explained that he had a ruptured gall bladder and was too weak to say anything more at this time.

"If I fly to Chicago, can I see him?" Evelyn asked in a trembling voice.

"Absolutely not," was the reply. "He is in very critical condition, and no visitors are allowed."

It was a week before Evelyn was to learn the details from Lou, as she stood at his bedside.

"Right after I called you from Denver, just as I was about to board the plane, I was hit with such excruciating pain that it totally immobilized me," he explained. "The emergency room doctors found a ruptured gall bladder. They wanted to operate on me right there, but I insisted they fly me back to Chicago. So I was packed in ice and flown directly to the hospital. They tell me that after the emergency surgery, my condition was so critical, the doctors saw no chance for recovery and sent for a priest who gave me the last rites."

"You were critical for three days," Evelyn cried, the tears running down her cheeks. "But you still insisted the nurse call me."

"I just couldn't leave this life without telling you that I loved you one more time," he said.

"But who is Ciucci?" Evelyn asked. "You said, 'Ciucci, I love you.'"

"I haven't the faintest idea," Lou replied. "But you were the only person in the world I was thinking about."

Back in Birmingham, Marie listened patiently to Evelyn's story during their coffee break, as they sat on the deck overlooking the office's garden court. "It sounds to me like you two are soulmates, or have been lovers in a past life," Marie said. "Nothing logical explains your relationship."

"That's not as silly as it sounds," Evelyn replied. "I've already thought about it, but haven't been motivated to find out. Maybe it's time I did."

"Just like that?" Marie laughed. "What do you do, call up God and ask him if you and ol' Lou have been together before in ancient Egypt?"

"No," Evelyn shrugged. "But I've done a lot of reading about reincarnation and I helped out on the support team when Dick Sutphen conducted his seminar in Atlanta. He teaches everyone to use self-hypnosis to regress themselves."

That night, Evelyn reviewed her notes about self-regression. She then unplugged the phone, turned out the lights and sat back in her recliner chair. The deep breathing relaxed her more and she felt a quietness of spirit begin to flow through her body and mind. "I call in my own guides and Masters and ask you to assist me in exploring my past. I want to better understand my relationship with Louis Santell. I want to know if he and I have been together in a previous lifetime."

Mentally, she counted backward from seven to one, visualizing herself going down, down, down, deeper and deeper asleep. She repeated the process and visualized a tunnel . . . a symbolic bridge from the present to the past. She was in the tunnel, tumbling backward in time, as the impressions began to come in.

"Tell me every detail," Marie demanded the following morning.

"It's not a simple story that I can easily relate," Evelyn replied, "but my initial impressions were of the Roman era. Although he looked very different, Lou was a Roman soldier, dressed in long robes and sandals. I was a woman and he was bringing me before the Council, but for what purpose I don't know. I have no idea what act I had committed, if any. But I knew that I loved him. Maybe that was the crime, I don't know. When in the presence of the Council, he remained at attention and totally ignored me. I remember someone calling me 'Ciucci.' But later, after the verdict, his eyes were so filled with love. There was just so much love in his eyes and emanating from his presence that I can't begin to describe it verbally."

"Well, what was the verdict? What happened?" Marie was almost beside herself, spilling her coffee in her eagerness as she leaned forward to stare into Evelyn's eyes.

"I don't know, Marie, I wish I did. The impressions were so vivid, it was all so real, but I didn't seem to have any control over what was coming in. I mean, I couldn't ask questions and receive answers. Maybe I could have if I knew more about what to do and how to do it. I'm sure a good regressive hypnotist could direct the process and obtain a lot more information."

Marie wasn't satisfied. "Okay, Evelyn, so you've been together. But why can't you be together in this life?"

"I don't know, but it must be our karma. Maybe we didn't appreciate our relationship in the past, so in this life, we are in a position of cherishing every moment we have."

"Don't you think you could change it if you wanted to?" Marie asked.

"No, I don't," Evelyn replied sadly and looked away. She knew, deep in her heart, that circumstances would never change.

In the fifth year of their relationship, Lou developed prostate cancer. Over the next two years, he had a series of three operations in an attempt to stay ahead of the deadly disease.

During the Christmas holidays in 1984, he was in the hospital again. Sitting with Rupert on her lap beside the crackling fireplace in her living room, Evelyn spoke across the miles to her Chicago lover. "Lou, do you realize it's been seven years we've been conducting this long-distance romance? Very few relationships could withstand the rigors of Ma Bell for that long."

Lou laughed in response, but told her it hurt when he laughed. "Monkey, I've never loved anyone like I love you. Maybe your belief in reincarnation explains it. Catholicism certainly can't. I feel like I've loved you forever, and I know I'll always be with you."

Shortly after midnight on January 12, 1985, Evelyn woke from a sound sleep, choking. No matter how hard she struggled and gasped for air, she could not breathe. In desperation, she pulled herself erect in bed to observe Lou sitting in a chair a few feet away. She caught her breath and sat trembling, her hands clutching her throat. Lou was looking at her with an expression so loving, it immediately calmed her down and brought tears to her eyes.

In the morning, she learned that Lou had died at 12:23 A.M. He was found seated in a chair with a newspaper spread over his lap, and a peaceful expression on his face.

September 1986: Evelyn talked Marie into attending a local class in the spiritual nature of man. Though reluctant at first, Marie consented. "But I'm still a skeptic," she reminded Evelyn after the first class.

The second evening of the class, Evelyn noticed the fragrance of *Halston 12* in the room. "Are any of you men wearing *Halston 12*?" she asked. Of the eighteen students, five were male, and all shook their heads in denial.

"Why in the world did you ask that?" Marie whispered. "I don't smell anything."

"It's the only cologne Lou ever wore," Evelyn replied. "I swear I smelled it a moment ago. Maybe I was mistaken."

Several weeks later, the class instructor introduced the concept of direct contact with the spiritual world through the technique of a trance circle. "I will choose one of you to sit in the middle, and the rest of us will form a circle around you. I'll then ask everyone to breathe deeply until I direct an altered state of consciousness and we combine our energy to draw in a loving spirit who is willing to share with us."

"How will he share?" asked a woman in the front row, anxiety obvious in her voice.

"Through impressions he directs into each of your minds," answered the instructor. "You'll be seated with your eyes closed, in a trance state. If you receive a strong thought, visual impression or feeling, I want you to speak up. Please wait for a quiet moment so you aren't all talking at the same time."

"Will it work?" asked a middle-aged man doubtfully.

"It always has," replied the instructor. "Evelyn, would you be willing to sit in the middle of the circle?"

"Yes, I guess so," she said, raising her eyebrows as she glanced at Marie.

As Evelyn began to breathe deeply, she thought about Lou. Naturally, she hoped that if it worked, Lou would come through. She craved assurance that he was all right. Because of his strict Roman Catholic upbringing, she wasn't certain things on the other side had turned out exactly as he had expected. Most of all, Evelyn wanted to reassure Lou that she still loved him.

The room was silent except for the audible sound of deep breathing. Evelyn was feeling light-headed when she noticed a gentle movement, like soft, warm air stroking her left cheek. It was such a familiar gesture. Whenever Lou was deeply moved, he always stroked her left cheek in a circular movement—soft and caressing.

"Yes, Monkey, I'm happy and I love you." The voice came from one of the men in the circle behind Evelyn. She shivered in response. "It's beautiful here," he continued. "You can stop worrying about me now."

Marie's voice was next. "I know now that I loved you even before I met you. You were right about past lifetimes, my love."

"We will always be together," said someone else. Then another spoke, and another. All around the circle, they spoke of things that had no meaning for them— things that were pieces of Evelyn's life. The words related to specific dates, times, and places. And Evelyn awoke drenched in tears of joy.

The following day, a red, circular area was obvious

on Evelyn's left cheek. "Looks like you were sun-burned there," Marie said, still somewhat shaken by the experiences of the previous evening. Three days later, the red area peeled off like a sunburn.

I talked with Evelyn in February 1987. She married after Lou died and today her name is Evelyn Bales. She explained that she and Lou still have contact. Sometimes it is a brief awareness upon awakening in the morning. "I realize that Lou has been with me all night," she explained. "He watches over me both day and night. I've had various psychic readers tell me that they see this man hovering over and around me, watching over me. And the first quality they mention about him is his devotion and love for me. Often they have been able to accurately describe his physical appearance as I knew him in this lifetime."

"Are you at peace with the relationship?" I asked.

"Oh, yes. I know now, without a doubt, that love is the strongest force in the universe. Even if Lou and I were destined to love and live apart in this lifetime, to learn our respective karmic lessons, we have a love that has survived the ultimate separation . . . death."

CHAPTER

9

Ann Palmer's Centerfold Love

The Saturday morning drive from Newport Beach to Simi Valley was a relaxing break in Ann Palmer's never-ending search for movie and television roles. Her continuing role as a nurse on "General Hospital" provided a base, but her character was only cast occasionally.

Her appointment that day was to meet at a friend's house to take pictures of each other for new composite sheets. As Ann's sports car climbed the 118 Freeway out of the San Fernando Valley, the air began to clear and the urban landscape gave way to rolling hills, fresh and green from the March rains.

Margie was also an ex-model and once-in-awhile actress who now lived alone in an aging ranch-style house situated on several acres of beautiful land. Ann had often tried to talk her into moving back to West Los Angeles, but Margie liked the quiet life and wanted a place for her kids to come home to.

"Being as mature as we are, we do understand the need of angles and soft lighting, don't we, my dear?"

Ann joked from behind the camera as she finished the second roll of 36 exposure Tri-X.

"If that doesn't do it, it will be the fault of the subject, not the photographer," Margie responded. "I'm going to make some dinner. If you want some photographic inspiration, Ann, there are a stack of magazines over there on the bookshelf.

"Some inspiration," Ann said a few minutes later as she entered the rustic brick and barn wood kitchen carrying a copy of *Playgirl*. She waved the open centerfold of a nude male over the sizzling wok of vegetables. "Isn't he incredible?"

"He looks stuck on himself," Margie said, stirring the contents of the wok with one hand as she sipped a glass of wine with the other. "But you have had more experience in such matters than I," she giggled.

Ann poured a glass of wine for herself. "No, I mean it, Margie. This guy is everything I've ever fantasized about finding in a man. It says here he is single and works in L.A."

"What could he possibly have that all your famous actors, singers, and athlete lovers didn't have?" Shirley asked, as she took the magazine from Ann. "Hey, this issue is six years old. Where did you find it?"

"Under the stack of *Popular Photography*. And that would make him a bit older and wiser than he is here. H-m-m-m-m."

"Good Lord, Ann, you really have chosen to work through the fairy-tale, prince-and-princess role in this lifetime, haven't you?" Margie said. Her voice was sharp and probing.

"I know, I know. I'm always looking for Prince Charming . . . the perfect man. My soulmate! But I've never claimed my attitude to be healthy or well-adjusted, Margie," Ann laughed, as they sat at one end of the large, dining room table.

"How many times have you thought, 'He's the one'?" Margie asked. "I remember the rendezvous with the head of the TV network. He was a prince, wasn't he? And so was the paranoid pot head from Phoenix. And then there was . . ."

"Got it!" Ann sighed, laying her hand on Margie's arm. "But don't you feel that the other half of you is out there, and someday you're going to find him?"

Margie smiled as she twisted the stem of the wineglass between her fingers and shook her head. "No, Ann, I feel like a happily divorced woman about to celebrate the big five-O, and glad to have the alimony to live like I do." She gestured toward the beautifully furnished living and dining room, the walls covered with original Western art. Beyond the patio doors was a swimming pool framed by the far mountains. "I guess I'm content with reality, Ann. Your life is glamorous and exciting, but it seems to generate more loneliness and frustration than satisfaction."

"I'm just not willing to settle for a frog . . . an ugly man. They say kiss a frog and a prince will appear. No way! I want to see a prince on the outside who is also a prince inside," Ann said. Her voice echoed her longing.

"Inner and outer beauty, huh?" Margie smiled. "The perfect mate." She picked up the copy of *Playgirl*. "Take it with you."

That evening, at home in Newport Beach, Ann wrote a quick note to Alan Graham, in care of *Playgirl*. She described herself as a beautiful, mature, tall blond, and explained she was interested in metaphysics and did psychic counseling on the side. As she sealed the letter, she thought, "I know you won't reply, but, then again . . . what if you do?"

Two weeks later, Ann made the following entry in her diary: "4/14/81–10:40 P.M.—The teenager in me is alive and well. This morning Alan (centerfold) Graham called. What a spectacular day! The Columbia space craft returned to earth this morning—a perfect flight. Going to L.A. tomorrow morning; will meet Alan at his apartment for lunch. Could he be gay? I have myself together and I am not counting on anything. *Anything* would be a bonus. The fantasy I've been living since Alan called this morning has been a welcome 'up.' If it has no finish or completion I can handle it. But I'm getting so tired of tests. How I would love to feel fulfillment!"

"Why did I write, 'If it has no finish or completion I can handle it'?" Ann wondered as she reread the page.

Promptly at noon, Ann climbed the steps of Alan's apartment building. As she rang the bell, awaiting the gate to open, she chastised herself for being so excited.

Alan answered the door, clad in a skimpy black bathing suit. "I hope it's all right with you?" he said, looking down at his attire. "Lunchtime is the only time I have to tan."

Ann didn't miss his obvious examination of her. "Perfectly all right with me," she said, scanning him from head to toe. He was handsome, 6'3", with curly black ringlets—Adonis come to life.

For the next two hours they sat on the patio deck, talking nonstop. Lunch was forgotten. "He's interesting, intelligent, uptight, and inhibited . . . and I love him," Ann thought, attempting to be attentive. "He is also at least seven or eight years younger than I am."

"I've got to get back to work," he explained. "Can I call you?"

"Please do," she replied in her most sensuous voice.

After waiting an agonizing month for a phone call that never came, Ann called Alan. "Oh, I'm sorry," he said. "Right after I met you I ran into an old flame and we rekindled our romance."

"Well, you obviously have some karma to work out with this woman, so call me when it's over. I'll still be here," she said matter-of-factly. Putting down the phone she thought, "We'll be together someday."

In the year and a half that followed, Ann dated, falling in and out of love with a musician, but she never stopped thinking about Alan Graham. In October 1982, she sold her Newport Beach home and moved back to Los Angeles, opening an office in the 1500 block of Westwood Boulevard. Acting jobs were few and far between, so she devoted all her energy to psychic counseling and past-life regressions.

An attractive mailer announcing her office opening was sent to friends, associates in the movie/TV industry, clients . . . and Alan Graham. Three months later, on January 10, 1983, Alan called at 11 P.M. They made a date for Sunday evening. The following is Ann's diary entry, describing the date:

"What a fun and awkward time! We had dinner in Westwood and went back to his apartment. After waiting two years, I was ready to go along with his every sexual desire (within reason). But he awkwardly put his arm around me while we discussed our individual needs from the opposite sex. It was rather adult, but I felt like a teenager through it all. As uptight as he was, eventually he agreed to a backrub. He removed his shirt and lay on the floor . . . gorgeous . . . but so tight and tense. While I massaged his back he explained his need for establishing friendship first, instead of rushing into meaningless sex. When I left, I told him, 'If you're really serious about friendship and it's not because you are not attracted to me, I am willing to go along with it all.' "

Their dates usually consisted of Ann going to

Alan's office and waiting for him until he reached a stopping point. They then went to his apartment, had dinner, and returned to the office. While he worked, she waited.

"Alan, there has to be more to life than this," Ann insisted, as they shared a bottle of wine on the couch. The top buttons of his shirt were open and she twirled his chest hairs as they talked.

"You mean sex," he replied, in a cool tone.

"Yes, among other things. I'd really like to make love to you. We've been seeing each other for several months."

"I just don't enjoy the same kind of sex that most people do," Alan said, avoiding eye contact.

"I'm open to just about anything," she said, meaning it.

The following is from Ann's diary, April 15, 1983: "I think Alan is testing me and my reactions somewhat. I have never known a man to be so obsessed by huge breasts or who enjoys masturbation more than intercourse. He wants me to watch him masturbate while he reads porn or watches X-rated videos. Although this has become a regular part of our lives, we have yet to make love. He is totally unconcerned with my needs. The thirty pounds I lost is rapidly coming back, and I think my body turns Alan off."

Diary entry, May 11, 1983: "I am determined that love will eventually win out for Alan and me, but I went out with Robert last night and we made love until dawn. It was wonderful, but I don't feel anything but physical lust for any of my other lovers. Yet I always ache to have Alan. I guess a part of him is better than all of other men."

Diary entry, June 19, 1983: "We finally had complete sex together. Maybe it was because I waited so long, but it was tremendously satisfying. I know this is the real beginning of our relationship."

The rolling hills of Simi Valley were brown and the leaves of the oak trees were orange and golden when Ann pulled into Margie's driveway. "Come on in, Ann. Brunch is almost ready," Margie shouted from the kitchen window overlooking the parking area.

"Cherry crepes and whipped cream, plus bacon and eggs. You're certainly not going to help me lose any weight, are you?" Ann grumbled happily, scanning the beautifully displayed buffet for two.

"I haven't seen you for months, love. Are you resolving your sexual frustrations with food?" Margie asked, patting Ann on the thigh as they sat at the table.

"I know, I've gained it all back and then some," Ann said, as she considered taking two crepes or three. "As usual, my love life is a mess."

"Why don't you let go of it, Ann? I can see that it's going nowhere. The mere mention of Alan's name generates hostile responses from the rest of your friends. Why can't you see it?"

"Obviously, I'm hoping it is going to change," Ann replied, shrugging her shoulders. "The crepes are great, Margie."

"Don't change the subject. Give me the latest rundown on you and Alan. And don't leave out any of the sexy stuff."

"I wish there was something sexy to relate," Ann said, as she stirred a teaspoon of sugar into her coffee. "Ever since we finally had sexual intercourse, he seems scared to death of me. I've managed to seduce him into real sex a few more times, but he seems to equate intercourse with a committed relationship, and he just isn't ready to commit.

"Sometimes I leave him alone for weeks. He never calls, and I eventually find some excuse to go by his office or call him. He never totally rejects me. I know he has a weakness for Mrs. Field's cookies, so I drop them by, or fix a special dinner and deliver it to his office."

"Pursue, pursue, pursue," Margie said, slowly shaking her head.

"Maybe it's the problem with kids. With my hysterectomy, I'm out of that game. He says he really wants to have children."

Margie just stared at Ann with an expression of mock disgust. "When you are together, what do you do?" she asked.

"I hate to tell you," Ann said, biting her lip.

"Tell me," Margie demanded.

"Well, he works seven days a week, night and day, so I help him out by cleaning his apartment and office. Organizing everything . . . you know. I'm a pretty damn good maidservant, but I don't mind—it's a chance to be together. How else could I spend time with him?"

"Gawd, Ann, I just want to shake you back into reality. There is no excuse for such a weird obsession, unless it goes back to those past lives you think are so real."

"You're right, Margie," Ann sighed, her tone apologetic. "I know the relationship is sick, but I seem helpless to do anything about it. Maybe I should be regressed."

"Do it," Margie said. "Anything that might bring you out of this absurdity has to be worth a try."

Diary entry, April 23, 1984: "I finally experienced my first past-life regression in search of ties with Alan. Wow! Matt conducted the session, which was extremely emotional. I cried and got very upset, but it

134

was worth it. And it makes sense. Our first life together was in Egypt, several thousand years ago. I was the daughter of a scholar, a man important in the political system. My father adored me, so his enemies kidnapped me and took me to a slave market. I was sold to a man who delivered me to a Persian ruler (Alan); I became one of his many wives. It seems he wanted the intelligence of Egypt in his lineage, and I was soon pregnant with his son.

"I saw very little of my boy and had little motherly attachment. I felt used like an animal for reproductive purposes. Accustomed to intellectual conversations, the library and mind-stretching games at home in Egypt, I withered in this Persian harem. The women knew nothing and cared about nothing except how to make themselves beautiful and how to please their master/husband. So I ran away, again and again. Each time my husband would send his men after me, to bring me back.

"Obsessed with returning to my father and Egypt, I felt my son would probably fare better as his father's favorite child, if I were gone. Eventually, my running away became such an embarrassment that my husband told me, 'I have done everything I know how to do to please you. If any of my other wives had done what you have done, I would have executed them. If you run away again, I will not send my men after you, and you will surely die in the desert.'

"Without his men coming after me, I knew I could make it, but I was wrong. Being small and frail, I fought a losing battle with nature. As I lay dying in the sand, I regretted my actions and thought of my husband. *'If I ever get back to him, I will never leave him again. I vow this upon my sacred honor. If I ever get back to him, I will never leave him again.'*

"Maybe the power of that vow has carried forward

several thousand years? I've scheduled another regression session with Matt next week."

Diary entry, May 1, 1984: "Matt conducted a scan regression in which we quickly explored many more lifetimes I've spent with Alan. It is almost too much to accept, but I sense the reality of it all.

"In France, we worked together as a priest and nun. I had the rare gift of healing in that life and was even sent before the Pope in Rome. Alan was a priest and was very protective of me. One day we were in the countryside, nursing the sick. On our way back, we were caught in a heavy rainstorm. We took shelter in a barn, and the storm continued on into the night as we huddled together to keep warm. He began to gently stroke my face in the darkness and I responded by putting my arms around him. When I felt his arousal I couldn't help myself, and neither could he.

"Being a nun was my parents' idea because of my healing ability. It wasn't something I desired to do. After the affair in the barn, I became pregnant. My priest-lover was defrocked and left the church, horrified at the outcome of physically sharing his love with me. I simply withdrew from the world, and never attempted to heal others again."

An awareness of the karmic aspects of the relationship changed little for Ann until May 1986, when Alan fell in love with another woman. "She's an airline stewardess who is far younger than me," Ann told Margie over the phone. "He loves to ski and her parents live in Colorado. What better place to ski, right?" Her voice was heavy with sarcasm.

"You hate skiing, Ann," Margie replied.

"I know I do. At least it appears that he *has* emotions now. Maybe he'll even be willing to spend a little money on her. He certainly never spent any on me."

"Ann, you know better than this. For over five years, you've been in love with a man who didn't love you. He should have had the guts to tell you, but for some strange reason, he seems to have been as helpless as you."

"Well, I have no choice but to let go of him now," she said in a choked voice.

"So, where do you go from here?" Margie asked.

"I'm not sure yet. Through all the past-life regressions I did with Matt, I realize, life after life, I have traveled alone much of the time, as a female striving to become complete and balanced. I guess that's what I need to work on again."

"I'll remind you of that the next time you call to tell me you're madly in love with some new hunk," Margie laughed.

The interviews with Ann Palmer were conducted early in 1987. The following letter arrived in May:

"Dear Richard, I recently bought a travel trailer and had planned to stay in an area like Sedona for a while and write, before attempting to conduct seminars in small towns. The night before I left Los Angeles, Alan came by to see the trailer. He told me he is planning to marry the stewardess. I told him I would always love him, and understood why I needed to experience the relationship as I did.

"No sooner was I out of Los Angeles than my trailer started acting up. I only made it as far as Victorville and was too paranoid to continue further into the desert. When the 'last straw' problem arose with the trailer, I threw up my hands and said, 'That's it. I'm taking the trailer up to Crestline for the summer.' I parked in the last available space on the mountain. Three days later, I met David. He's my own age and shares my interests in metaphysics, theater, and show business. He has a background as a writer and producer. Like me, he, too, is starting over, after many problems.

"When I regressed David, he went back to his first earth lifetime. Much to my surprise, his story dovetails with my own initial experience on the planet. Am I here to resolve another soulmate experience or will I take my act on the road as I planned? For now, I'm just settling in among the tall pines, planning classes, weekend retreats, and writing . . . and, for the first time ever, enjoying and sharing with a man."

10

Patrick and Gael Flanagan's Dharma

July 1982, Camelback Inn Ballroom, Scottsdale, Arizona: Gael Gordon, an attractive twenty-nine year old with a model's body and nearly waist-length, raven-colored hair, sat in the audience of the week-long Sutphen Super Seminar—an annual metaphysical event offering four workshops a day presented by leading New Age authors and holistic practitioners.

Author/scientist Patrick Flanagan was onstage speaking about how to develop and use psychic energy. In his late thirties, he moved rapidly around the stage to express points and diagram concepts. As one of the leaders of the "pyramid energy" movement of a few years before, Flanagan had written some successful books on the subject as well as developing a line of energy products. The audience of 250 was in rapt anticipation as he demonstrated how to build psychokinetic energy and then discharge it to move physical objects. Placing a straw across the top of a water glass, he stepped back a few feet and began to move his fingers at the straw like Merlin the Magician. Nothing happened on the first attempt, so he increased the intensity of his efforts. A few seconds later, the straw moved, then moved some more. The audience cheered and applauded wildly.

During the course of Patrick's lecture, he discussed ancient Hopi Indian prophecies; to demonstrate the secret fraternal handshake, Patrick asked for a volunteer from the audience. Gael raised her hand and was chosen.

"Are you sure you want to do this?" Patrick joked, as she stepped gracefully onstage.

"I'll try anything once," she replied, coquettishly.

A year later, Patrick would admit to Gael, "When you came up on the stage and I touched you for the first time with the sacred Hopi handshake, I thought you were the most beautiful woman I'd ever seen. I felt like I'd always known you."

After the seminar, both Patrick and Gael returned to their respective homes in southern California. Patrick lived in Brentwood on the western edge of Los Angeles, and Gael had an apartment in a rustic house in the Angeles National Forest. It was through her work and research with crystals and precious stones that she had met the apartment owner, one of the country's leading importers of gemstones. He offered Gael a recently vacated apartment in a house filled with millions of quartz crystals and precious stones. Here, in this quiet environment of tall pine trees and a creek that ran through the property a few feet from the door, Gael spent her days in meditation, writing and researching crystals.

"You're obsessed with crystals!" her friend, Mary Windsor, said. "They ought to be your middle name."

"Crystals are the whales and dolphins of the mineral kingdom. They're our friends," Gael responded.

"Whales and dolphins, huh?" Mary chided, raising her eyebrows. "Well, speaking of strange things, I just met the greatest psychic. You've got to let him do a reading for you."

"He doesn't happen to have a beard and levitate tables, does he?" Gael asked.

"Yes, he does. How did you know that?" Mary asked, in surprise.

"A dream. I saw a man like that in a dream I had a few months ago," Gael replied with a faint tremor in her voice. "When can I meet him?"

"I'll bring him over Sunday afternoon," Mary said, stroking one of Gael's favorite crystal balls fondly on her way to the door. The two women walked down the stone path to Mary's car. "Considering I have to drive through the creek to get in here, what happens when it rains?" Mary asked.

"No one comes in or goes out," Gael laughed.

"See you Sunday . . . if it doesn't rain," Mary said, then carefully guided her car into the flowing water, twenty feet across the creek, and out.

"Jim Banner, Parapsychologist" read his card. He was a short, bearded man in his middle forties, dressed in a slightly baggy suit. Gael recognized him immediately from her dream. "How much do you charge for your readings?" she asked, offering a cup of herbal tea.

"I won't accept money from you, but if you want to give me a crystal in exchange, I'll wear it always," Jim responded, looking around the sparkling room in awe. "I don't know if it is you or all these crystals, but I've never experienced so much energy in my life."

Gael settled herself comfortably on the couch across from the psychic while he self-induced a light,

141

altered state of consciousness. Mary excused herself to take a walk in the pines.

About ten minutes into the reading, Jim asked, "Who is Patrick?"

"I don't know anyone named Patrick," she said. She paused for a moment to think. "Oh . . . Patrick Flanagan?"

"Can you capture his essence in your mind?" Jim requested. "Picture him as vividly as possible—how he looks, how he moves, how he talks."

To her surprise, Gael easily remembered Patrick, as she mentally relived the handshake experience.

"Yes, that's him," Jim continued, seeming to respond to Gael's subjective impressions. "You will meet again and will cross the sea together. You will help him discover something that will greatly benefit mankind. It has to do with water and the rejuvenation of the body. You will do great things and you will be together for the rest of your lives. I'm getting incredibly strong impressions as to the importance of this discovery the two of you will share."

"When will this happen?" Gael asked. She struggled with a dawning uncertainty.

"He has to resolve some problems with others in his personal life before he can realize his true destiny," Jim said, as he rubbed his temples.

The rest of the reading accurately touched upon several other aspects of Gael's past and offered some general advice for the future. She paid the psychic with a beautiful quartz crystal and filed the recording of the session away with her other metaphysical cassettes.

"What did you think of the reading?" Mary asked the next day on the phone.

"He was very good, but I have no way of knowing much about his predictions in regard to Patrick Flanagan. I really liked Patrick when we briefly met

142

onstage last summer, but I know nothing of his current relationships. I guess time will tell."

In April of 1983, Gael received an invitation from The Sutphen Corporation to be a speaker at the annual seven-day seminar. "We'd like you to lecture on and demonstrate crystals," said the letter of invitation.

"Are you going to accept?" asked Mary.

"Sure, why not?" Gael responded. "I used to lecture all the time back East on crystals, metaphysics, and health. I'm a little out of practice at public speaking, but I'm sure it will come back quickly."

Three months later, Gael was standing near the Super Seminar registration area when Patrick Flanagan, also a speaker, walked up to her. "Are you a Taurus?" he asked. "Did you originally live in the Northeast?"

"Yes, and yes," Gael replied in a chuckling voice. "Do I get a prize for answering correctly?"

"Yes, as a matter of fact you do. You win me!" His voice, deep and sensual, sent a ripple of awareness through her body and mind. They both laughed and Patrick continued, "A psychic told me you are going to be my future wife." He looked at Gael, smiled and shrugged his shoulders, shyly.

Gael looked at him with amused wonder. Recovering, she said lightly, "This is a bit sudden—could you give me a few minutes to think about it before I accept?"

Over a candlelight dinner, Patrick explained that three months earlier he had received a psychic reading from a woman in Los Angeles. "She said I would meet my life-mate at a seminar where I would be lecturing; the woman would be a few years younger than me, a Taurus and originally from the Northeast. Also," he paused significantly, "she is supposed to have beautiful red highlights in her long dark hair. When I saw you again today, I knew in my heart you were the person the psychic was talking about."

"What else did she tell you?" Gael asked, a smile on her face as Patrick ran his fingers through her hair and down her arm. Her skin tingled at his touch.

"She said you would give me the love, support, and commitment that no other woman could provide. That we would marry and move to a mountainous area and live happily for the rest of our lives."

"Do you believe everything psychics tell you?" Gael asked, shaken, as she sipped her wine. Her attempts at levity were fading, and her voice was a tremulous whisper.

He laughed in response and shook his head happily. "No, but I've been lecturing all over the country, and I must admit I've been on the lookout for a potential soulmate with long, reddish-tinged dark hair."

"Any other prospects?" Gael asked. Patrick exchanged a smile with her, then shook his head. "You're not the only one who listens to psychics," she said, her voice shakier than she would have liked. "But my psychic mentioned you by name."

Soon after the seminar Gael joined Patrick for the weekend—a weekend from which neither returned to their former life. During their first three days together, they explored the unknown. Using self-regression techniques, they simultaneously recalled their past lives together as Count Alessandro and Countess Serafina Cagliostro. Research revealed the Cagliostros to be controversial, eighteenth-century metaphysicians who greatly resembled Patrick and Gael. There were several other parallels between the two couples, who were separated by more than two hundred years.

Alessandro Cagliostro was an alchemist, herbalist, and healer. Through the assistance of Saint Germain, the Cagliostros were initiated into the Order of the

Knights Templar and soon displayed their knowledge as Rosicrucian adepts. Working on their own, the couple formulated rejuvenating elixirs. They developed a plan for initiation and enlightenment which consisted of a forty-day retreat that began with the full moon of May. It included a natural diet featuring elixirs designed to remove body toxins.

More of Gael's psychic reading proved true when she and Patrick traveled "across the sea" three months later to become man and wife. A special ceremony in the King's Chamber of the Great Pyramid of Giza, the wedding was scheduled to coincide with an auspicious astrological alignment that occurs only once every several thousand years: the Pleiadean Alignment.

The alignment lasted for three days. On the first day they were married. Their second night was spent in the King's and Queen's chambers, where they were initiated into the secrets of the Great Pyramid. On the third night they climbed to the apex, fifty stories above the desert floor, spending the entire night alone in the light of the full moon.

After visiting the sacred temples of Egypt and Greece on their honeymoon, the Flanagans returned to the United States. They moved to a remote mountainous area in northern Arizona, where they purchased a secluded home on several acres. After their initiation in the Great Pyramid, they felt a great need for seclusion, to meditate and fast. The attainment of the highest level of inner purity became their shared goal.

On the twenty-second day of their fast, both received vivid visions and a revelation about the nature of water as the primordial source of all life. Awakening from the trance-like experience, they went into Patrick's laboratory, where they began a series of experiments, resulting in the eventual development of a colloidal mineral water offering health-enhancing properties.

Mixing it with juices, they tested it by fasting for six-month periods. Friends' experiences supported their own, and research projects using the water with race horses, plants, animals, and athletes also proved successful. A co-authored book, *Elixir of the Ageless*, followed, and the water was released under the trade name *Crystal Vortex*™.

Dharma is generally defined as your duty to yourself and to society. Some people see it as their true purpose in life. It means following a course of action that is right for you. By following your dharmic nature, or self-nature, you will most easily evolve, and fulfill your commitment to the greater whole—mankind. Karma conditions you through all your experiences to create the character necessary to carry out your dharma.

It may be your dharma in this life to be a responsible householder and raise your family. Another person may have dharma which directs him into government work, a life of service work, or philosophy. It is my dharma to communicate metaphysical ideas to as many people as I can. It is B. J. Thomas's dharma to brighten the lives of millions with his beautiful music. It was Thomas Edison's dharma to serve mankind through scientific inventions that would enhance the lives of everyone on the planet.

Patrick and Gael Flanagan are a perfect example of soulmates with shared dharma in the areas of science and service. Though close friends, they live in almost total seclusion, so my wife, Tara, and I seldom see them, but we keep in contact by phone. Over the years I've often been the subject of Patrick's seemingly wild experiments which have served so many. (At age seventeen, Flanagan was listed as one of the top scientists in the country by *Life* magazine.)

"What are you up to now?" I asked in May 1987.

"The elixir book is being translated into Spanish, Japanese, Chinese, and German," Patrick said excitedly. "And a university study was just completed with the water. The tests indicate that it increases the nutrient uptake in plants by as much as four hundred percent."

"But what are you doing for excitement?" I prodded.

"Well, we managed to spend a night meditating with the crystal skull. And, Gael just adopted a wolf dog to add to our menagerie. That makes six dogs, two goats, three rabbits, a horse, six cats, four parakeets, and a very outspoken cockatoo. Life is always exciting around here."

11

Donna Gruber's Karmic Triangle

"I've been aware of Maria, my spirit guide, since I was a young child," Donna explained to past-life regressionist Bryan Jameison. "She has helped me out many times in this life. It was through her I learned I won't meet the man I will eventually marry until I am older. I'm thirty-nine now and I haven't met him yet."

"How can I help you?" Bryan asked, sitting with his back against the arm of his office couch. Donna sat at the other end, dressed in her United Airlines stewardess uniform. The warm glow of the late afternoon sun filtering into the room created the illusion of an aura around her long blond hair.

"I have the strongest feeling of predestination about this, and I thought maybe my past lives would be a clue to my future," she said, almost apologetically.

"Have you ever experienced past-life regression before?" Bryan asked.

"Yes, at a Sutphen Seminar several years ago. It was a powerful experience."

"Tell me about it," he said, reclining in a more comfortable position and placing his feet upon the coffee table.

Donna stared out the window at the San Diego skyline, attempting to remember. "It was in the 1600s, I believe, in a small Sioux Indian village. I was a young woman named Fawn. My older brother, Tall Trees, raised me. Our mother had been killed in a tribal raid, and our father died while on a hunting expedition.

"Tall Trees and I were very close. I would have been very happy to live out my life in his lodge, but when I was fifteen, our chief's son, Many Moons, decided to make me his wife. He said I would provide him with a healthy son. I should have been honored for I didn't even have a dowry. Instead, because of my deep love for my brother, I resented Many Moons' proposal and made a silent vow to never give him what he wanted.

"Soon after the marriage, I became pregnant. The elders predicted a boy and Many Moons was pleased. I, however, sank into a deep depression that greatly weakened my body. The baby was born dead. Many Moons blamed me for not being stronger. Secretly, I was happy that I hadn't provided him with a healthy son.

"Many Moons didn't forgive me for over a year, and I was seventeen when I became pregnant for the second time. This time I caught a fever and the baby was born prematurely. It was a boy, but he lived only a week. I died very shortly thereafter. My hatred for Many Moons was so intense, I think I willed myself to die.

"That's it as best as I can remember it, Bryan," Donna said, getting up and walking to the window. Beyond the buildings was the ocean. She couldn't see it but she could sense its tranquility, just a few blocks down the street.

"And neither Tall Trees nor Many Moons seem to be people in your present life?" Bryan asked.

Donna shook her head without turning around. "I asked about it at the time."

"All right, let's do another regression," he said. "I'll phrase the suggestion to say, 'If there is a man in your past that is destined to be part of your future, you will now go back to a lifetime you've shared.'"

Donna agreed and made herself comfortable, lying back on the couch. Bryan closed the blinds and turned his desk lamp to low. He then pulled a chair close to Donna's head and in a firm, soothing voice, began to direct her deep breathing. When the induction was complete and she was in deep hypnosis, he asked, "Can you speak up now and tell me what is happening?"

"I'm just outside by the fields," she replied in a noticeable Southern drawl. Her voice sounded younger.

"What is your name?" Bryan continued.

"Annalise Jones, and this is Jeremy Wilson. He's my best friend. He lives right over there."

"And where do you live, Annalise?"

"Virginia."

"What year is it? Do you know?"

"Of course. It is 1784."

"All right, I want you to let go of this now, Annalise, and I want you to move forward in time until something very important happens. And when you can, I want you to speak up and tell me all about it." Bryan closed his own eyes and brought his hand to his forehead, as if attempting to perceive Donna's subjective impressions himself.

"We're in a coach. Jeremy and I are married, and

he is going to teach in the West. When we get . . . oh, no . . . Indians. They're chasing us. They're chasing us. There are so many of them. Jeremy is holding me and he's saying, 'It'll be all right. It'll be all right.' " Donna began shaking as she reexperienced the anguish.

"What is happening now?" Bryan asked.

She didn't answer, so he asked again.

"I'm just floating, looking down at what happened. The coach went over an embankment, and Jeremy and I are just lying there. So is the driver and the other passenger. The Indians are crawling all over . . . it is dreadful. Dreadful! I think I'm dead."

"I want you to let go of this now. On the count of three, you'll be back in the present. You will remain in a relaxing, deep hypnotic sleep, but you'll be back in the present, remembering everything you just experienced. One, two, three. All right . . . take a deep breath. Relax, and listen closely to my words. You have just experienced a lifetime in which you were together with a man you are destined to love again in this life. If you have shared another lifetime together, I want you to go back to that lifetime now. I'll count backward from five to one, and on the count of one, vivid impressions will emerge from your subconscious to your conscious mind."

Donna smiled but didn't answer.

"Please speak up and tell me your name and where you are," Bryan stated, his voice warm and firm.

"My name is Margaret Marie Dundee, I'm fourteen and I live in Boston."

"What year is it, Margaret?"

"1874."

"Tell me about your life. I'd like to know about your family. Do you have any brothers or sisters?" Bryan asked.

"My mother is Amanda and my father is John. He

is in the import-export business. They wanted lots of children, but my delivery was so difficult for my mother, the doctor warned her not to have any more children." Donna giggled at this point in regression.

"What is funny Margaret?"

"Well, it's just that I'm an only child, and all my aunts and uncles tell me I'm spoiled."

"Let's move forward to something very important that will happen in the future. You're going to grow up a little. Time is passing. On the count of three, vivid new impressions will come in. One, two, three."

"I'm in love with David Hamilton. We met in school and he's so handsome. We fell in love right away. He asked me to marry him."

"Tell me more about David," Bryan said, making notes on the pad he held in his lap.

"He is two years older than I and his father owns the bank—the one closest to our house. David is going to learn the banking business and someday take his father's place."

"All right, Margaret, let's move on to something important that is going to happen in the future." Bryan completed the instructions and soon she was describing their wedding and the happy life that followed. In another progression, she relived the birth of her daughter. "We named her after my mother, Amanda Marie Hamilton. But David and I call her Mandy."

Bryan progressed Donna forward in time again, but this time she became very upset, necessitating the following suggestion. "I want you to fully understand everything Margaret is experiencing, and then in a moment, I am going to awaken you. You will be able to tell me about it, very calmly, without emotion."

Donna opened her eyes, looked at the ceiling and shook her head. Bryan handed her a tissue. Wiping the tears from her eyes, she said, "That was no fun,

Bryan," and clasped her hands together tightly in her lap. "Whew!"

"Can you talk about it?" he asked, looking at the notes he had taken.

"Sure," Donna responded, sniffling slightly. "When Mandy was about five years old, David was made president of the bank. I decided to surprise him at closing time, so we could go celebrate. I left Mandy with our housekeeper and walked the few blocks down the street to the bank. It was so real, I could even feel my long, hooded cape brushing my legs. It was late fall, and the air was chilly.

"Suddenly, I sensed someone behind me. Before I could turn around, I felt a knife plunging into my back. Then I was above my body, looking down. The man who killed me fled, but somehow I could read his mind. I knew that on a conscious level he killed me because I was attractive and would reject him. That's it," Donna said, looking directly at Bryan.

"I'd like you to go back into hypnosis and up into your Higher Self in an attempt to see how this fits together. Are you willing?"

Donna considered it for a few moments, then nodded as she laid back on the couch.

"In your Higher Self, you have total access to your subconscious memories, and superconscious awareness as to how they relate to your present life," Bryan explained. He then induced hypnosis and completed the slow counting ascension into the realms of higher mind. "All right, Donna, I now want you to perceive everything you can about the past lives and how they relate to each other and your present incarnation."

Two or three minutes passed before she spoke. "The man who stabbed me did not know me personally in that life, but it was Many Moons from the Indian

153

lifetime. We have been together in many, many incarnations, and always as adversaries. After the stabbing, upon first crossing over into spirit, I felt cheated at losing such a beautiful, happy life. But those wiser than I showed me how it was the hatred I had for Many Moons that drew him back to me, lifetime after lifetime. They explained that the only way to resolve a disharmonious bond is through love. I'd been told this many times before, but I obviously wasn't ready to let go of it. This time I listened and worked on it, in spirit and in an incarnation that followed. In place of my hatred, I now feel a warm and happy glow."

Donna took a couple of deep breaths before continuing. "Tall Trees, Jeremy, and David are all the same soul. I will meet him again in a few years. We will be married and will remain together for the rest of our lives in this incarnation. Many Moons, in another incarnation, was the leader of the Indian raiding party that caused our deaths in the coach. Plus, he stabbed me in Boston. My daughter Mandy in the Boston life is currently my spirit guide, Maria.

"There are some other karmic ties between these lives and the present. A few years ago, I had an overwhelming urge to buy an expensive replica of an eighteenth-century Victorian doll. Even with a broken kneecap the price was $150, but I felt I had to have her. In my Boston lifetime, Margaret was given a doll identical to the one I now own. She dropped the doll one day and broke its kneecap but continued to love her just the same.

"In my current life, I've always had a fear of being noticed. To be attractive meant something bad would happen to me. I've felt if I remained average I'd be safe. This is a false fear relating back to the stabbing."

* * *

Donna Gruber first attended a Bushido Training I conducted in Portland, Oregon, in the late 1970s. Since then she has often volunteered to serve on seminar support teams in cities wherever United Airlines flies. After taking professional hypnosis training, she developed her own techniques for past-life regression. Today, when Donna isn't flying, you'll usually find her conducting private regressions for people at her home in Aurora, Colorado.

In April 1987 I asked Donna about her past-life experiences, and her conclusions.

"My triangle?" Donna laughed. "Well, obviously, I am one of three souls who have come back together again and again to work out their karma. I think the situation with Many Moons is resolved. I sure hope so! Hopefully, Many Moons has also let go of his hatred of me, but even if he hasn't, I'm out of it. Next time, he'll be combined with another soul who has a karmic configuration matching his own needs. How do you see it?" she asked.

"Well, I contend that we are here on earth to learn to let go of fear and to express unconditional love," I replied. "It sounds to me like you're doing it. Sadly, we all seem to learn fastest through pain . . . which is usually by directly experiencing the actual consequences of our actions. In your case, hatred generated more pain until you finally saw the light and decided enough is enough.

"You accepted responsibility for the stabbing, Donna. When someone accepts karma as their philosophical basis of reality, their life changes. Neither God nor the Lords of Karma are responsible for our suffering. We are each our own karmic judge and jury, and there is no one to blame for anything. And the only reason we make our lives difficult is so we will learn faster."

"To restore our harmony, right?" she said. We both laughed.

"I don't have to talk basic metaphysics to you anymore, do I? You're even teaching it yourself now."

"Not formally, Richard. But when explaining karma to people, I find the 'pond and harmony' example communicates quickly. To throw a stone in a pond is a good example of cause and effect, which is karma. I am the cause, and the effect is the splash and ripples. And the ripples flow out to the edge of the pond and back until eventually, through the physical law of dissipation of energy, the pond returns to its original tranquil, harmonious state. Similarly, all our disharmonious thoughts and actions disturb the balance of the universe. And they will flow out and come back upon you until eventually you regain your original harmonious state, and karma is balanced.

"I think everyone on this planet is here because they want to return to a state of harmony. Most of them don't realize it but that's what is," Donna continued. "We each have free will to do it the hard way, through pain and fear. Or, I think we can do it the easy way, through love, grace, mercy, helping others and accepting them as they are. I don't know about you, but I'm ready to start doing it the easy way!"

"Agreed, Donna, agreed!"

CHAPTER

12

Zan and Nanciee's Revelations

October 1981: The 195 people at gate 38 of the Amsterdam International Airport had gathered together from all over the United States for the Egyptian tour. Zan Zerah had been hired as a photographer for the two-week adventure. She was a pretty woman in her early thirties, 5'7", with short dark hair. She was accompanied by her younger assistant, Elaine Powell. They had flown in from New York that morning with the assignment of capturing the tour events on stills and video for possible release as a documentary.

The job had fallen in Zan's lap. A San Diego friend of a Phoenix friend had suggested to the tour organization that they hire Zan. Her initial reaction to a two-week assignment in Egypt was less than enthusiastic, but when Elaine offered to come along, she accepted.

"Is that Nanciee Rogers?" Elaine asked, tapping Zan on the shoulder. "She seems to be in charge of the tourists."

"I don't know, I've only talked to her on the

phone," Zan replied, staring at the attractive blond woman. She was very slender, dressed in expensive clothing and jewelry; she appeared to be in her early forties. "Beautiful, isn't she? Flashy and beautiful."

"Down, girl! You've promised yourself never to get involved with a straight woman again. 'Tis to-o-o-o difficult, remember?"

"I know, Elaine, I know, but she almost takes my breath away," Zan said in a low voice as she turned away in an attempt to shake off the feeling of recognition. "Life would certainly have been simpler if you and I had fallen in love."

"And ruin a great friendship? No way! It was my karma to be there for you after you handled your heroin problem. Now I get to enjoy photography and advise you in your love life. Besides, *I'm* the one who is attracted to blondes." They laughed. Zan again focused her attention upon Nanciee, who was busily checking in the tour participants.

"I think I'm in love," Zan thought to herself. Her mouth curved into an unconscious smile.

The tour proceeded to Egypt. During the daily explorations of the pyramids, Zan used every photographic opportunity to get close to Nanciee. "But I never get to be alone with her," she complained to Elaine back in their hotel room.

"What is this intense attraction all about?" Elaine wondered aloud as she washed some clothes in the bathroom sink.

"I don't understand it either, Elaine. She's not my kind of woman. Nothing about it makes any sense. All I know is, for the last ten days I've been like a lovesick puppy dog." Zan lay back on the bed, staring at the ceiling in the dim light. Through the open window came the sounds of the Cairo street below, and the enticing aroma of highly spiced cooking.

158

"This is ridiculous," Zan continued. "You know how I can't stand being around smokers? I don't allow anyone to smoke in my apartment or car. Well, this evening I was up in Nanciee's room, along with ten or twelve others, and she was sitting on the bed chain-smoking. You could hardly breathe in the room. And there I sat at the foot of her bed, waiting for the hordes to leave."

"I think Nanciee loves you," Elaine said, poking her head through the bathroom doorway. "She doesn't know it yet, but you should talk to her."

"Elaine, I've come on pretty strong and I haven't received the slightest encouragement from her. You know I refuse to be manipulative, or play seduction games." Zan nervously moistened her dry lips.

"That's exactly why you need to talk very straight to her. Tell her exactly what you feel while you still have a chance. We go on to Israel and they return to the States in three days."

It was their last night in Egypt before Zan found the courage to talk to Nanciee. "I have to talk to you alone," she almost pleaded in Nanciee's ear as the group, returning from dinner, walked through the hotel lobby.

"Let's take a moment right now," Nanciee responded with a warm smile, taking Zan's arm and guiding her to the high wicker lobby chairs. The rest of the group went on, some to their respective rooms, others to the hotel bar. The only exception was an Egyptian man, who had been following Nanciee all week. "He's as lovesick over her as I am," Zan thought as she seated herself beside Nanciee. The Egyptian sat directly behind them.

Neither the timing nor the location were ideal. At first, she had difficulty saying the well-rehearsed words. Slow shadows from the ceiling fan, circling above, danced across the expectant look on Nanciee's smiling face. Zan felt detached and far away as she heard her voice speak of the feelings in her heart.

"What happened?" Elaine asked, anxiously looking up from a week-old copy of the *New York Times* when Zan returned to their room.

"I don't believe it," Zan exclaimed, throwing her hands in the air. "You know me, Elaine. I'm articulate and express myself well. I told her about my affection for her. I was really straight."

"And . . ." Elaine prodded, attempting to hurry the story.

"And, when I was done, she put her hand on my knee, squeezed it and said, 'If you meet the Buddha on the road, kill him.' She thought I was looking for a guru, I guess. It all went right over her head. She had no idea what I was talking about."

"You really don't think she understood?"

"No, absolutely not," Zan replied, as she slumped into the overstuffed chair by the window. "Straight women aren't worth the hassle. Do you know she has four grown kids, ages twenty-eight to thirty-four?"

"I know you're in love, and Nanciee will still be in New York when we get back. I'll talk you into calling her then," Elaine said, tossing a pillow across the room at her friend.

Two weeks later, in Manhattan, Zan and Nanciee spoke several times on the phone. Months later, Nanciee would refer back to the conversations: "I'd say things like, 'I really care, I miss you, there's a hole in my life when you aren't here.' Then I'd get off the phone and wonder, 'Why did I say that? What's going on?' "

Back at home in San Diego, Elaine continued to encourage Zan. "I'm telling you, she loves you. Go see her at home in Arizona. If nothing else, you've been invited to stay at her house while attending the seminar with Brad Steiger and H. N. Banerjee next month. Go!"

"I'll go, but she'll probably have ten other people staying at the house," Zan said.

Nanciee's house was a contemporary Spanish design, surrounded by palm trees on a two-acre lot in the foothills, overlooking the Paradise Valley section of Scottsdale. Zan wasn't surprised by the eclectic furnishings from all over the world, accented by Egyptian decorative pieces, Persian rugs, and original works of art. Fresh flowers decorated every room. The dining area opened onto a patio and a large, tiled pool. In the distance were the mountains that surround the Phoenix Valley.

As expected, there were many other guests and Nanciee approached Zan with a request, "I've used every spare nook, cranny and bedroll in the house. I'll have to share my bed and I don't feel comfortable with anyone's energy but yours. Would you mind?"

"Oh, ah, not at all, Nanciee."

Winter nights are cold in the desert, so Zan wore her long johns and stayed well on her side of the bed. "There is no way I can come on to this woman," she thought as she lay quietly in the darkness. "It has to be mutual, or it won't work."

On the third day, shortly before she was scheduled to return home, Zan managed to talk to Nanciee alone. The following afternoon, over lunch in a San Diego restaurant, Zan explained to Elaine what happened. "This time I was very, very clear. I told her I was in love with her. I made sure she knew it wasn't the guru kind of love. And she responded by saying, 'I understand, dear, I understand.'"

"Then what?" Elaine asked, putting down her fork and staring into Zan's sad brown eyes.

"Then nothing! I sensed more to it, but there was no real response."

"I knew it!" Elaine exclaimed. "She loves you. Now you've *got* to go back to Scottsdale again when she doesn't have a house full of people."

"For God's sake, Elaine, I'm not self-destructive. This has gone beyond silly. I'm so in love it's all I can think about, but I'm not going to keep doing this."

"Trust me, she loves you," Elaine laughed. "If you were really clear in your communications, Nanciee is processing it all now, and she is probably just about completing the denial phase."

"I really believe that Nanciee is one of those rare women who has never questioned her sexuality," Zan said. "I know she has lesbian friends, and she certainly carries no prejudice, but I doubt if she's ever had a bisexual fantasy."

"Until now," Elaine whispered, reaching across the table and tapping her index finger on Zan's hand.

Nanciee and Zan now talked on the phone several times a week, but the messages from Nanciee were as mixed as before. "Can you come to Scottsdale for a weekend?" Nanciee asked. "I'm closing my office in town and moving it into my third bedroom here at the house. The weekend after next, I'll be ready to sit back and relax around the pool."

Zan accepted the invitation and arrived in Scottsdale to find a second house guest, Teri Ochoa, a joint friend from the Egyptian tour. Nanciee said, "With the office in the house, I only have two bedrooms and Teri is using the guest room. Are you willing to share a bed with me again, Zan?"

By late evening, the three women were a little high

on the wine they had drunk. When Teri began to dance with a rose between her teeth, Zan started snapping Polaroids. "Good Lord, look at this one," she exclaimed. "Nanciee, you were in the background with your back to me when I took this of Teri. But look at it. One side of your body is right there while the other side is just an outline, with the kitchen window, faucet, and sink showing right through your body."

"I guess I'm just half here on the earth," Nanciee laughed, looking closely at the picture.

"It's perfectly clear, and it's obvious you didn't move," Teri added, looking over Nanciee's shoulder. "It sure spooks me. You'd better find your soulmate, Nanciee, so you're whole again."

The subject weighing so heavily on Zan's mind seemed to be blocked by Nanciee whenever it started to surface. Although she had an enjoyable weekend, Zan was not receiving responses she was comfortable with, so she made no sexual advances.

The weekend visit became a week-long visit. On the third night, as Zan lay in the darkness, eyes wide open as she attempted to sort things out, Nanciee asked, "Would you hold me, Zan? Just hold me."

The two women fell asleep in each other's arms. The following night, Nanciee seduced Zan. "Of course, it didn't take much seducing," Zan admitted. They spent the rest of the week getting to know each other, talking until dawn when they would fall asleep, exhausted after long periods of lovemaking.

"I've had heart problems in the past," Nanciee explained. "And each time Zan slept in my bed, I'd lie awake, my heart pounding, unable to sleep. I thought it was angina attacks, but it was the anxiety of my repressed feelings."

Teri shared their excitement in discovering each

other. "I just wish I could capture on film the way you two look at each other every time that song plays. What is it, 'Long Ago, So Clear' by Vangelis?"

"It has to be our song," Zan responded, and Nanciee agreed with a nod and smile.

"Look at this," Nanciee said to Teri and Zan one morning as they were having coffee beside the pool. "Last year I decided I wanted and deserved a fulfilling, growth-oriented, spiritually committed relationship with someone who would make me happier than I had ever been in my life. I wrote down my manifestation list for the exact type of person I desired. See if this list doesn't fit Zan to a tee?" She handed the page to Teri. "You'll notice the only thing I left off was the physical sex of the person I desired to draw into my life."

The three women laughed until tears rolled down their cheeks as they read Nanciee's affirmations. "You're going to live together, aren't you?" Teri asked. They both nodded.

"Nothing is really holding me in San Diego. I can free-lance anywhere," Zan said. "Being the metaphysical entrepreneur that she is, Nanciee needs to be where her business is established. We've decided to drive to San Diego next week to gather my things and break the news to Nanciee's children. They all live in the general area."

"That sounds like an interesting project," Teri responded. "How do you think they'll take it?"

"Very well, I hope," Nanciee said, glancing at Zan and smiling. "They're all used to their mother's crazy ideas and activities by now."

"This revelation may be a little more traumatic than mom discovering a new guru," Teri said, patting her chest.

They left Scottsdale in Nanciee's Mercedes shortly after sundown. The sunroof was open and beautiful New Age music from the stereo system filled the night. The lights of the city gave way to the desert, and moonlight softly silhouetted saguaros with their arms lifted to the heavens. Thirty miles out of Phoenix, they left Interstate 10 and took 85 to Gila Bend, then Interstate 8 toward Yuma. An hour and a half into the six-hour drive, the strains of "Long Ago, So Clear" filled the car.

> Once . . . we did love,
> How we chased a million stars,
> And touched as only one can,
> Once . . . we did play,
> How the past delivered you . . .

Nanciee slowed down and pulled off to the side of the road. She reached over for Zan's hand. Zan took her hand and brought it to her lips, kissing gently, then put her arms around Nanciee. The women embraced as the song filled their souls.

When the music faded, they leaned back in their seats, eyes raised to the night sky. "I love you."

"I love you, too. Wow! Look at that!" A shooting star flashed across the sky, directly overhead. It was quickly followed by another, then another. They sat silently for a few minutes. Without further discussion, Nanciee started the car and pulled onto the nearly deserted highway. Wellton was a gas stop, and as the lights of San Diego began to appear on the western horizon, the first light of dawn was appearing behind them.

"Something is wrong," Nanciee said, glancing at her watch. "Something is terribly wrong."

"What?" Zan responded, coming fully alert in her seat.

"I've driven this highway from Phoenix to San Diego

a hundred times. It's a six-hour trip. We only stopped for ten or fifteen minutes to listen to the song and watch the shooting stars, but nine hours have gone by."

"Then we must have been in a time warp," Zan joked, "because we certainly didn't go to sleep."

"No, we didn't," Nanciee said, again looking at her watch.

They awoke in Zan's apartment late in the afternoon and made slow, lingering love for more than an hour. Afterward, Zan inserted the Vangelis tape in the bedroom stereo and lay back to relax in the orgasmic afterglow. She folded her pillow behind her head, and as the strains of "Long Ago, So Clear" filled the room, her eyes began to flicker. Raising her hand to her head, she heard Nanciee whisper, "Oh, my God," and slump into the pillow beside her. There was a sensation of dizziness as the bed dissolved and they cast off their physical forms—simultaneously shooting through space, united, traveling at an incredible speed, feeling purposeful and alive and leaving a fiery trail as they plummeted toward the earth.

Nanciee later explained, "The trail was me. As I came to earth, I veered to the left and became aware that the other half of that trail was also me, and it veered to the right. Wild as it sounds, I know the other half of the trail was you, Zan."

"I had exactly the same experience," Zan replied. "Only I veered to the right and I also knew we had been one."

"Could it be that somehow the song triggered an emotional response to something we experienced, but don't remember, during the time warp last night?" Nanciee asked, almost to herself.

The Rogers children were concerned about their

mother's decision, but very supportive. For the next four years Zan and Nanciee lived together and shared a soulmate relationship. In September 1986, responding to inner directions, they moved to Quilcene, Washington.

After exchanging several letters, I had an opportunity to interview Zan in my office in May 1987. She was in town to work with an agent on the marketing of two metaphysical screenplays and a New Age video she had recently created with Nanciee and New Age musician Steven Halpern.

"How is it working out in Washington?" I asked.

"We love it," Zan replied, enthusiastically. "We're both hermits at heart, and this is a dream come true, although we've certainly had our trials."

"What kinds of trials?"

"The fire, for one thing. Nanciee had an incredible amount of 'stuff,' and I'd done my own share of collecting over the years. Almost everything we owned was packed into the moving van, and before it was delivered in Washington, the truck caught fire and we lost it all. I was carrying all my video, film, and negatives, so they were saved, but that was all. Of course, we figure we created that monster."

"What do you mean, Zan?" I asked, curiously.

"Well, Nanciee and I had both been talking a lot about simplifying our lives without doing it. And we made statements such as 'Let's make sure we never move all this again.' We figure the universe heard us and said, 'Okay, I'll fulfill your request!'"

"Any other trials?"

"I don't know if you are aware of this, Richard, but Nanciee has had brain surgery twice in the last two years. It's only in the last six months that she has been up and around again. But even this has served us both, for it has been a lengthy process allowing us to reaffirm our love and release all kinds of old stuff."

"Nanciee can see the positive, even in experiencing brain surgery?" I asked.

"Oh, yes, in many ways. Probably the most powerful changes were in regard to self-image—she never really liked her physical self, and didn't want to be here on this planet. I guess she felt she didn't really belong here, that it was all some kind of mistake. Her illnesses gave her many opportunities to leave, but instead she decided to stay. She saw how abusive she had been to herself over the years in areas such as diet and behavioral patterns. Today, as a result, she really likes herself and is more excited about life than ever. She'll probably offer metaphysical workshops at the ranch someday soon."

"Tell me about the ranch."

"Well, we have a beautiful home on twenty-five acres. Two-and-a-half acres are our private lake, stocked with fish. We have a well, a 3,000-square-foot garden and we're almost self-sufficient."

"Isn't that an awful lot to take care of?"

"It sure is, but Nanciee's youngest son and his wife have just moved up to handle all that. They purchased a mobile home and moved it to the property."

"Is your desire for self-sufficiency related to the belief that there will soon be major earth changes?" I asked.

"Yes, it is," Zan smiled.

"One final question, Zan. In a recent letter, Nanciee told me, 'The love Zan and I feel and experience every day of our lives is so complete and so profound, mere words fail to properly convey all that our commitment is to each other. It truly encompasses every facet of our lives.' I think that is a beautiful thought, after being with someone for five years. Do you agree?"

Zan looked at me shyly, smiling, and said, "Oh, yes."

As a past-life therapist and seminar trainer, I am often asked the metaphysical view of homosexuality. From a karmic perspective, it is simply a life-style choice—no different than choosing to be heterosexual, bisexual, male, female, black, white, yellow, or to be born in Kansas City or Moscow. The soul decides upon the sexual orientation for the growth potentials it will provide. Different periods in history have offered very different growth opportunities for gays. Homosexuality was commonly accepted in Greece, and many regarded the love between two men to be the highest form of love. Compare that to the attitude of most Americans toward gays in the '30s and '40s, the liberal attitudes of the '70s, and the nightmare of AIDS in the '80s.

The karmic lessons involved could cover the entire spectrum of life, from learning to be true to who you are, to experiencing an introverted position in a judgment-oriented society.

Metaphysics teaches "what you resist you become—if not in this life, in the next." Resistance is fear that needs to be resolved. So another reason for being gay in this life could be your resistance to homosexuals in a past life. By directly experiencing homosexuality, you would come to understand your resistance and thus transcend your fear.

CHAPTER

13

Helen Fredericks' Physical and Balancing Karma

"How do you like the fast lane after living in Montana?" Dale asked the new receptionist at Associated of Los Angeles, a wholesale electrical house on East Olympic Boulevard.

"I haven't seen much of the fast lane yet," Helen responded. "I started looking for a job before I even finished unpacking my boxes in the apartment."

Helen liked Dale Fredericks. He was funny, and he made her feel at ease in her new position. He was also tall and sinewy with thick tawny hair.

Helen sat behind a large glass window, looking out on the showroom of fixtures, switches, and wiring. One of her jobs was to call for assistance when Dale was overwhelmed with customers. Her initial impression was that he was about eighteen years old. He was twenty-five and single. She was twenty-four and married.

They began talking at coffee breaks and over sack

lunches. "You're the easiest person to talk to that I've ever met," Dale said, finishing his lunch. He spun a frisbee on his index finger.

"Tell that to my husband, will you?" Helen said. "We have the worst communication in the world."

"I can't imagine your not being able to communicate," Dale said in surprise.

"Oh, I communicate," she said. "Too much, as far as he's concerned. He refuses to talk about our problems. His answer to any disagreement is, 'If you don't like it here, there's the door.'"

The men at Associated spent part of every lunch hour playing frisbee. Helen enjoyed watching, both the game and Dale. "I know your dad is the manager of receiving. Is that why you are working here?" she asked him one day, as they ate lunch on the loading dock, waiting for the rain to stop so the frisbee game could begin.

"Yeah, when I got out of the navy in 1975, they offered me a job. I didn't manage to save much in the service, so I moved back in with my folks."

"How does that work for you?" Helen asked, a note of surprise in her voice.

"The three of us lead a very structured life because my mother, Ann, has a hard time accepting changes," he said, raising his hands in a gesture of futility.

"What do you mean, 'structured'?"

"Oh, let's see . . . every single Monday night we bowl, after which we have Jell-O and coffee while watching the eleven o'clock news. If we are home in the evening, we have a snack exactly at nine. Maybe beer and chips. If it's beer, my mother purchases three beers that afternoon for the occasion."

"What about having a couple of extra beers in the fridge?" Helen asked, jokingly.

"Oh, no," Dale said. "She plans everything by the day, and only exactly enough for the day. If we have a guest, the women get one serving and the men get two."

"Doesn't it get to you?" Helen asked.

"I'm good at detaching," he replied.

Three months after beginning the job, Dale confessed to Helen just how special he felt she was. "I know it sounds really dumb, but I drove out to your house on Saturday and just sat there in my car, hoping to see you."

"What would you have done if I'd seen you?" she asked in reply.

"I don't know," he said. "I just wanted to see where you lived," he said shyly.

"Didn't you say you were going down to Manhattan Beach to visit friends on Sunday?" Helen asked. Dale nodded. "What a coincidence! I have a girlfriend who lives in Hermosa and she invited me down the same day. Why don't we meet late in the afternoon for a drink on the pier?" Dale agreed, and Helen quickly called her friend to see if she'd like a Sunday visitor.

Helen and her husband separated soon afterward, and she began dating Dale. The more they saw of each other, the more Dale's mother, Ann, resisted Helen. "You two see each other all day at work. Why do you have to be together on evenings and weekends?" she asked Dale, angrily. Helen always responded warmly to Ann, going out of her way to appease the older woman, but to no avail.

"Why don't you move out?" Helen asked Dale one day when he complained of another argument with his mother over her.

"And move in with you?" Dale asked, his watchful eyes intent upon her reaction.

"Well, I really don't like living alone," she said, smiling and touching an index finger to his lips.

When Dale broke the news to his parents, Ann created such a scene that Dale began to doubt his own mind.

"Maybe we should hold off a while?" he asked Helen.

"Dale, I'm not going to sit around on evenings and weekends waiting for your mother to allow you to see me," she replied, her lips thinning with displeasure. "If we aren't going to move in together, I think we should date other people."

"We're moving in together," he said. The date was March 26, 1977.

Helen and Dale were married on January 5, 1978. For the first fifteen months after the wedding, they were together twenty-four hours a day. "We work, play, shop, eat, sleep, and even shower together. It's terrific," she told a friend. "And most important of all, we *communicate*. We became best friends while falling in love."

The only flaw in the Fredericks' life was Ann. "Why does she hate me so much?" Helen repeatedly asked Dale.

"I don't know," was his response. "But you aren't any fonder of her than she is of you."

"But that's only because of the way she treats me. I can't face your joint birthday party this weekend. Why do you both have to be Leos?"

"The party will be in a public restaurant. She won't act up in front of others," Dale said, confidently.

During the birthday party dinner, the conversation turned to the subject of abusive parents. Ann talked about a woman she knew who had a large family and treated them badly. "At least I never killed my babies," she said in a low voice, looking hatefully at Helen.

"What do you mean? Did the woman you know kill her babies?" Ron, Dale's father, asked, in confusion.

"No, not her." Ann replied, continuing to stare at Helen. Ron shook his head, more confused than ever, and looked at his son helplessly.

"Do you hate me because I can't have children?" Helen asked loudly, her body shaking with emotion.

"Your wife has no respect for my feelings," Ann said to Dale in an angry voice.

"What about my fucking feelings?" Helen screamed in response, the alcohol loosening her tongue. "I didn't just decide to have abortions for the hell of it. Both times I attempted to carry a child, I was told that my heart could not handle it and I would die. The hospital committee almost demanded the abortions."

"Don't talk back to me like that, young lady," Ann said threateningly as she arose from her chair.

"I'm not listening to any more of this," Helen said, glancing at Dale. "I'm going home. Are you coming with me?"

"Yes, come on," he replied, taking Helen's arm and turning to leave. Ann quickly moved around the table, blocking their exit, and shoved Helen as hard as she could.

"I ought to knock some sense into you," Ann snarled. "You always take him away from me!" She then sank back into a restaurant chair and began to sob, "I'm never going to get to be a grandmother. I'm never going to get to be a grandmother."

It was a year before Dale talked to his parents again, and a year and a half before Helen was willing to see them in March of 1982. In January 1987, Helen explained, "Ann and Ron moved to Kentucky. We see them occasionally, and we get along all right now. I accept Ann the way she is as a result of my becoming interested in reincarnation. Around the time of the restaurant fight, I had gone to the store to get a paper, but I didn't have enough change to get one out of the dispenser. So I went inside and bought a paperback book, *You Were Born Again to Be Together*. I've never had the nerve to ask for change without buying something.

"The book opened the door to reincarnation. Then I saw an ad in the *Los Angeles Times* for a Sutphen Seminar. I tried to talk Dale into attending with me, but he wasn't interested. He did encourage me to go, however, and he liked the changes that resulted from my seminar experience. I became more self-confident and stopped saying 'I'm sorry' all the time.

"From then on, no matter how long the seminar was or how much it cost, Dale always found a way for me to attend. And the more I grew, the more he supported me. I shared my past-life experiences in hypnotic regression with him and he agreed that it made logical sense. As my interest in the subject intensified, he encouraged me to write about my experiences.

"I learned of many lifetimes in which I have been together with both Dale and Ann. Two incarnations seem to be directly related to the physical and balancing karma I am experiencing in this life.

"The most recent lifetime was during the Civil War. Ann and I were friends and both in love with Dale. He married Ann, but a few years later had an affair with me, causing me to become pregnant. When she found out, she paid a man to rape and kill me. He stabbed me through the heart with a bayonet.

"Physical karma is a carry-over of a physical affliction from one life to the next. I was wrong in having sex with my friend's husband, and she was wrong in having me murdered. In both cases, karma was incurred that must be balanced. In this life, I was born with a hole in my heart. Because of this, I can't have children, and Ann can't have grandchildren due to a physical condition she caused over a hundred years ago. That's balancing karma in action. I am not assuming there isn't more to it, because other lifetimes are also involved.

"My most vivid past-life, hypnotic regression was of being a young woman living in Scotland during the Middle Ages. The year was 1525. My wealthy parents arranged a marriage with the son of an equally wealthy family in the next county. The wedding was to take place when I reached the age of fourteen.

"My mother died when I was very young. I was the only daughter. My father, an intelligent, scholarly man, taught me and my brothers to read and write. He encouraged me to learn and study many subjects because I showed great interest and a natural intellectual aptitude. Generally, women of my status learned the social graces, needlepoint, weaving, and other genteel pastimes. It was highly unusual for me to be so learned and well read. At this historical time, it was considered unfeminine for a woman to apply herself to intellectual pursuits.

"At the age of fourteen, I was married; part of my dowry was a large country estate which had been in my family for generations. It contained stables, gardens, many bedrooms, a library, parlor, study, formal dining room, kitchen, and nursery wing.

"Having been raised with as much freedom as my brothers, I was very headstrong. At first, I viewed running a household as another challenge and set about learning to do it to the best of my ability. But I soon became bored with such simplistic endeavors, and let a capable housekeeper direct the staff. Eventually, I restricted my involvement to menu planning and party arrangements.

"When I was sixteen, I had my first child, a daughter, followed by a son, and another daughter, but I was not interested in the children. The challenge they posed wasn't intellectual enough for me, so most of their care was assigned to the servants. This allowed me to spend most of my time in my library—reading, writing, and studying. I had no interest in anything else. Even the social activities which once interested me were now boring. The ladies of my social circle were no more interested in my attempts at sparking their interest in scholarly pursuits than I was in their inane conversations.

"My husband complained, constantly and bitterly, that I neglected him, the children, and our estate in my obsession with reading and writing. The more we fought, the more I retreated to my library, where I hid reclusively among my books.

"Finally, my husband exploded. He declared that I could no longer read, write, or study. From that day on, I was to be a proper wife. I would know my place and keep it. He went into my library and destroyed all my writing materials, throwing them into the fireplace. He even burned my desk and chair. Finally, he burned all the books I had collected over the years. When he was finished, he shoved me out of the room, slammed the heavy wooden doors and locked them, pocketing the key.

"I was devastated, and fled numbly to my bedchamber, my mind reeling. He had destroyed everything I cared about, and he would die for it; he and his precious children that he cared so much about. With all of them out of the way, I could do as I pleased with no further bother.

"That very night, I crept quietly into his bedroom and stabbed him to death. I was very cold and calculating about it, knowing I must kill him first or he would prevent me from killing the children. After the last breath bubbled through the gaping wounds in his chest, I rushed into the nursery wing and quickly murdered the children, first the eldest daughter, then the middle son and the youngest girl last of all. A knife is silent and they died quietly.

"The servants discovered the bodies in the morning. When they rushed into my room to see if I had also been murdered, they found me sitting in a chair in the middle of the room, covered with blood, the knife on the floor at my feet. I was slowly writing the reasons for the murders on a scrap of paper my husband had overlooked in his destructive zeal.

"My sentence was life in a tiny cell, furnished only with a pallet on the floor. The judge proclaimed no one was ever to speak to me, or to visit me as long as I lived. I was not allowed to read or write anything, and when they discovered I was using my finger to write words in the dirty cell floor, they cut off my finger. Many long, hopeless years later, I died of starvation.

"My husband in that lifetime is Dale in this life. My oldest daughter in that life is Ann today. When I first related this past-life regression experience to Dale, he reminded me of how when we were first together, I constantly asked him if he felt neglected while I was reading, or writing.

"Maybe it also explains why he has been so supportive of my growth needs in this life. The regressions may also explain why Ann said, 'You always take him away from me!' "

* * *

In discussing the case with Helen, I said, "It's a good story to show how two or more past lives can generate a combined balancing effect in the present."

"To me," she said with a note of resignation in her voice, "it is a good story to demonstrate how we program ourselves to learn by directly experiencing the consequences of our actions."

CHAPTER

14

Glenda Carlisle's Karmic Relationships

"If you're ever going to get over Charlie, you've got to go out and get involved with people," Kay said to Glenda over the phone.

"I don't want to meet anyone else," Glenda replied flatly. She looked out the apartment window to see children playing in drifts of orange and yellow leaves.

"You'd let your best girlfriend go to a wild Halloween party all by herself?" Kay asked, hoping to induce guilt. "If some man takes advantage of me, it will be your fault. Besides, the psychic told you about a new man coming into your life. 'You'll know him by his eyes.'"

"If I went to the party, it would only be for you. You wouldn't want that?" Glenda said. Her tone wasn't quite serious.

"You bet I would. I'll pick you up at seven thirty. The club opens at eight. Come up with a great costume."

All afternoon, as Glenda attempted to create a costume, a thought repeated over and over in her mind:

"Tonight is important! Tonight is important!"

Glenda answered the door, dressed as a gypsy. "Al-l-l right!" Kay exclaimed. "You do make a cute little spellbinder—pretty enough to cast a sexual spell over any man in Salt Lake City."

"You're quite convincing as the pirate you really are," Glenda laughed. "But look at my brown hair. Gypsies have blue-black hair and piercing brown eyes."

"With that low-cut blouse, they'll never notice your hair, believe me. Come on, we don't want to miss any opportunities," Kay said, as she bounced down the front porch stairs. Glenda followed her friend into the blustery night.

There were few people in the club at 8:15. Black and orange crepe paper streamers arched between the posts, and cardboard cutouts of pumpkins and witches were taped along the bar and around the windows. Glenda and Kay ordered wine and sat at a table near the dance floor. On the stage the band members were setting up their instruments and conducting a sound check. "Will you please wipe that sad, 'I miss Charlie,' look off your face," Kay said, tapping her glass on the table to emphasize her words.

"Oh, it's not really Charlie. It's everything. Anyway, I'm the one who left Phoenix and came back here to start a new life, remember?" Glenda replied, exaggerating a huge smile.

"How did you ever meet old Charlie the race car driver, anyway?" Kay asked, twirling her wineglass as she scanned the people slowly beginning to fill the dance club.

"My father was a dentist in Kansas City and Charlie's mother was his assistant. Our families spent a lot of time together socially. If ever there were two opposite people, it was Charlie and me."

"So you grew up together, huh?"

"I had an incredible crush on him when I was a freshman in high school, but his parents moved to Phoenix, Arizona. In the following years, Charlie would pop in for unexpected visits whenever his job or schooling called for trips through Kansas City. There was always a strong attraction between us. But, as you know, I married someone else. I didn't see Charlie again until 1982 when he was on a national racing tour."

"And you still had the hots for him?" Kay interjected rhetorically.

"I guess you could say that. The attraction was almost unbearable, but since I was married I called it an early evening. A few months later, he sent me a letter. It was just a general 'How are you, what's new?' I sensed something behind the words, though I couldn't quite put my finger on it. My divorce was in process when I heard from Charlie again. His letter arrived on the day I was leaving Kansas City to move in with my sister Sherry in Malibu."

"So you instantly called him and said, 'Let's make up for lost time, Charlie baby!'" Kay said. She was laughing as her eyes followed a well-built man in a breechcloth and body paint. "Would you look at that!"

"You are the horniest woman I've ever known, Kay."

"It must be a reverse reaction to all the good Mormon vibrations in this town. Anyway, so did you?"

"Did I what?"

"Call Charlie."

"No. Once I was settled in Malibu I sent him a letter, not really expecting to hear from him for months. Three days later, he called me from his home in Phoenix. We made a date for lunch the following day and he drove all night to get there. I left work at 11 A.M.

to meet him and didn't return home until 4 A.M. the next day. It was the beginning of the most intense love affair I've ever experienced."

"Oh, I already know that, my dear," Kay said in a low, silvery voice as she seductively pumped her hand up and down the stem of the wineglass.

"Kay!"

"Exactly what did you do to screw it up?" Kay asked, dodging Glenda's swat at her arm.

"I'm convinced it was destined to end as it did. During the first six months of the affair, we spent a fortune on long-distance phone calls, plane tickets, and gas. I drove my MasterCard over the limit, but I didn't care about anything except how to spend another weekend with Charlie. It was an addiction."

"Was he as hooked as you?" Kay asked, serious for a moment.

"At the time I thought so, but he never said 'I love you.' It was taboo, without ever being discussed. So I finally wrote him a letter stating exactly what I felt— how deeply I loved him and, no matter what happened between us, that I would always feel this way. We were on our way to Mexico for the weekend when I gave him the letter. When we arrived, he was very distant. Eventually, he told me that he loved me too, but it confused him.

"We started to grow farther and farther apart. In a last-ditch effort to save the relationship, I moved to Arizona to manage one of his used appliance stores that supported his racing habit. After living there for six months, seeing him less and less, I knew it was time to step out of his life," Glenda said. Tears suddenly welled up in her eyes.

"That was over a year ago," Kay said, leaning over to stroke Glenda's hand. "It's time to let go and have some fun again." The club was packed full now and the band played earsplitting rock and roll. Late arrivals were standing two and three deep at the bar and lining up along the walls.

Glenda looked up to see the Grim Reaper standing beside her. "How have you been? Long time, no see," he said in a deep-timbred voice.

"We're not quite ready for the Grim Reaper just yet," Kay replied, a noticeable lack of enthusiasm in her voice.

"Well, if you're not ready to die, are you ready to dance?" he asked, bowing to Glenda and extending his hand. He was wearing a mask and full body costume, so she had no idea what he looked like. Nodding acceptance, she took his hand. He led her across the crowded dance floor to a clear area near the far wall.

"My real name is Jeff," he said as he gathered her into his arms. His eyes were dark and unfathomable behind the grotesque mask. Her skin tingled at his touch. Glenda had a sudden flash of memory. "You will know him by his eyes." She looked away and buried her face against the corded muscles of his neck. His breath was warm and moist against her cheek and she felt a strange peace.

The phone rang ten times before Glenda answered it the following morning. "I hope you got a ride home," Kay said. "After the midnight shuffle number, I couldn't find you again."

"I couldn't find you to tell you I was leaving with Jeff," Glenda replied, shaking her head. She rubbed her temples with her free hand. "It's like I've always known him. I still can't believe how comfortable it felt. Apparently, he felt the same way. He shared himself very openly, which is something he claims he never does."

"I don't believe it. I was open to score, you weren't. You did and I didn't. There is no justice in the world. I'm going to take another cold shower. Good-bye!"

Glenda was still smiling as she brewed the coffee. She was just finishing her first cup as she dialed the phone. "Kay, how was your shower?" The buzzing sound of a vibrator laid against the mouthpiece on the other end of the line hurt Glenda's ear. "Sorry I interrupted you, Kay," she laughed in response. "But it's your turn to go somewhere with me. No excuses, I'll be over to pick you up in an hour. Have fu-u-u-n!"

"Let me get this straight," Kay said, standing in the doorway of her apartment. "You want me to go with you to some airy-fairy meditation class? I don't believe it. I'm going back to my vibrator."

"No, you're not," Glenda said, taking her by the arm. "I'm carrying too many pounds on this short frame and it's time I did something about it."

"Oh, good! We're going to meditate the fat away because Glenda has a new love interest!"

"You could reduce those love handles a bit yourself, my friend," Glenda said, backhanding Kay's thighs as she led her to the car.

The class was held in a second-floor aerobics studio on the edge of downtown. Susie Bowers explained the exercise. "Once you're in an altered state of consciousness, I will direct you to visualize a particular behavioral pattern or trait separating from yourself and materializing in a form you can directly communicate with. I don't want you to force this visual impression, just let it form naturally on its own."

The seven students relaxed on the exercise mats and closed their eyes. Soothing New Age music filled the room as Susie directed a slow, yoga-breathing exercise. Body relaxation followed, and as though from far away, Glenda heard the instructions.

Her head rolled slowly from side to side as she

attempted to perceive the vision. "It's there. I can almost see it," she thought. "It's . . . it's just a penis. A giant pink penis. Good Lord, this is Kay's vision, not mine." She started to laugh, then stopped. "Why do I feel so threatened by a penis?" A terrible fear engulfed her. "It's going to make me disappear," she thought, experiencing a flood of perplexing emotions which erupted into compulsive sobs.

Noticing Glenda's anguish, Susie whispered in her ear. "Explore the source of your feelings. You can do it."

As Susie spoke, the visions expanded before Glenda's inner eyes. Instantly, she knew she was in England, in a dark park near a pond. Then, as if she were watching a movie, she saw a man grabbing her . . , then another man and another. Her clothes were ripped away. She couldn't scream. A huge hand clamped her mouth shut while others forced her legs apart. The grass was wet on her back. She squeezed her eyes shut until the black pain between her legs was gone. There was only a golden light, drawing her away. "Why, why, why?" she heard herself screaming as the scene began to dissolve into a mist.

"It's all right, child," said the concerned voice of her spirit guide. "You chose to make a karmic sacrifice. Those men had already raped and murdered six other young women, but because of your murder, they were apprehended. This was also a lesson for your guardian who has much to learn about love. He cared deeply about you, but would not allow his emotions to cloud the logic of his mind. He treated you with cold indifference. Your sacrifice assisted him to learn to love while he had the chance."

Within the vision Glenda finally found her voice. "Why did I feel such anger directed at me?" she cried.

"Your fiancé feels a great rage. He blames you for allowing this to happen," was the reply.

"I don't understand, am I in the past or the present?" Glenda asked.

"Both, my child. Your fiancé in the English lifetime is Charlie in your present incarnation. When you were murdered, he blamed you for leaving him and he never forgave you. Although a young man at the time of your death, he spent the rest of that life alone and bitter. The incident left you both with unresolved karmic fears. Charlie was attracted to you in this life because of the love you've shared, but he fears any serious involvement—especially with you, because he doesn't want to be hurt again. You have been using your excess weight as a shield of protection. Subconsciously, you feel if you aren't attractive, you won't be raped and murdered."

"What about my guardian?" Glenda asked.

"Your guardian from the English incarnation is Jeff today," was the reply.

Glenda responded slowly to Susie's awakening count. She opened her eyes to see Kay, lying beside her, raise herself on one elbow and lean over to whisper, "I had a great nap, how about you?"

Jeff and Glenda were married in 1985. Glenda is the sister of my seminar coordinator, Sherry Rueger, whom she came to visit in Malibu in the spring of 1987. On a Sunday afternoon, while relaxing on Sherry's deck overlooking the Pacific, I asked Glenda about her current relationship with Jeff.

"We have a great friendship and Jeff is learning much more about expressing love, but he always maintains an emotional aloofness that tends to support what my guide explained in the meditation."

"Are you happy?" I asked.

"Yes, I am. We may not share intense passion, but we are growing together and we both love each other very much."

Both Marcie McGyver and Glenda Carlisle were gang raped and murdered in a past life. At first I wasn't going to include two case histories with such similar backgrounds. But, after considering the similarity in cause events though different in effects, I decided the cases offered a unique opportunity to demonstrate karma in action.

Since they both died in the same way, why was the effect for Marcie a preoccupation with death, while Glenda gained weight, subconsciously hoping to go unnoticed by rapists and murderers?

There is no way to know for sure why karma manifests as it does without knowing the complete karmic history of an individual—something impossible to realize. But we can speculate on the effect of various factors. First, there is always the possibility that either or both of the women lived other lifetimes after the rape/murder and before their current incarnations. If so, new influential factors have been introduced. In other words, they may have improved or worsened the situation, depending upon what was experienced.

Marcie seemed to experience more pain in leaving her husband than from the tragic ending of her life, thus her fear of death relates directly to the fear of losing her husband again. Glenda may not have carried the same depth of feeling for her fiancé, so her primary pain reflects the horror of the death battle. Our future is always being written by how we respond to the events in our lives.

15

Thai Wright and the Policeman

"Bakersfield Police Department," said the official-sounding voice on the other end of the line.

"My name is Thai Wright, and you've got to do something about my neighbors," she said quickly, agitation obvious in her voice. After obtaining her address, the desk officer instructed Thai to calm down and explain.

"My neighbors are rock and rollers who play electric guitars all night long. I've asked them politely for a week and a half to turn them down, and they say, 'Sure, sure' but nothing happens. The more stoned they get, the louder they play. Now they're out on their porch with a rifle trying to shoot down the advertising balloon that floats above the Circle K store on the corner."

"An officer will be right there," was the impersonal reply.

The tall, blond policeman introduced himself as Michael Dennison. "Your call was out of my assigned area but I felt impelled to respond," he said to Thai, his watchful blue eyes scanning her as well as the room. She explained the situation with the neighbors, indicated their house, and watched from her kitchen window as the officer crossed the lawn to the white stucco house next door.

The neighborhood was like most other postwar housing developments in southern California. The blocks of small houses varied little in design, with each displaying a "swamp cooler" on the roof beside the television antenna. Palm trees, long ago grown to maturity, lined both sides of the street. The policeman had gone inside the house and everything was quiet. Thai glanced at the indoor/outdoor thermometer mounted above her sink. It read ninety-nine degrees, at 1:30 in the morning. She thought about the handsome officer and the electric reaction she had experienced when their eyes met.

"Enough of that, Thai," she said to herself. "You've only been divorced for six months and if there is anything you don't need in your life, it's another man wanting a one-night stand." Her thoughts were interrupted by the doorbell.

"I don't think you'll have any more problems," Michael Dennison said. "They've got marijuana growing in the living room. I told them if there was another complaint, I'd bust them on both counts." His smile brought an immediate softening to his features.

Thai hesitated momentarily. She swallowed hard, trying to manage a proper answer. "Thank you. Thank you, officer."

"Michael," he corrected her. "I'll call you at least once a week for a few weeks to make sure everything is okay."

"I would appreciate that," she said, beginning to close the front door. "Good night, Michael."

Thai leaned against the closed door. Crossing her

arms across her chest, palms down on her shoulders, she took a deep breath and realized she wasn't wearing a bra. Her nipples were erect, showing through the thin tank top. "I wonder what he thought of me?" she said out loud, stepping in front of the full-length hallway mirror. Her long, black hair was tumbled casually over her shoulders and her cutoff jeans exposed attractive legs, well tanned by weekends spent lying on the back-yard lounge, writing poetry. "I could write a poem about him and I don't even know him," she thought, switching off the light.

Michael called. Each week after checking on the neighbor situation, he always found an excuse to chat about other things. On the third week he asked Thai out to dinner, and she accepted with mixed reactions. "You have to understand, I haven't dated anyone since my divorce," she explained. "I'm very nervous about this."

"Do you have any idea how nervous I was about asking you?" he responded. They both laughed.

A month later, Thai spoke with Arleen Graham at the Insight Bookshop, in preparation for a past-life regression. Thai, a longtime student of Arleen's Expanded Awareness classes, wanted to see if she had ever shared a lifetime with Michael. "From the moment I met Michael, I wanted to embrace him and hold him, but it didn't make sense," Thai explained. "On our first date, he kept trying to look into my eyes. Every time he'd look at me I'd get embarrassed like a schoolgirl and look away. That's not like me at all. I just felt as though we'd known each other a long time. Then, a couple of weeks later—after we'd made love for the first time—he admitted that he wanted to look deeply into my eyes on that first date. He explained that when he answered the police call that night, he instantly felt like he knew me, I mean *really* knew me.

But he didn't go into it any further, and I never brought up reincarnation."

"Well, I want you to lean back, relax, and make yourself completely comfortable," Arleen instructed. "Let's find out if a tie really exists."

Thai quickly responded to Arleen's soothing voice and felt her body begin to relax, her mind quickly following. All her questions and thoughts seemed to slowly dissolve as her attention focused upon a gentle, swaying sensation. She seemed to be spinning and the voice was far away: "If indeed you have ever shared a lifetime with Michael Dennison, you are now going back to that incarnation. On the count of one, you'll be there."

Thai heard the numbers dreamily as the blackness faded into gray. She was detached, but she was there.

"Will you please tell me your name?" the distant voice asked.

"Elizabeth Michaels."

"Can you tell me where you are and what year it is, Elizabeth?"

"Cheyenne, Wyoming, and it is 1860," she replied softly.

"Tell me what is happening, Elizabeth."

"I'm sitting under a tree. Charles is approaching me, leading his horse. He's wearing military dress and . . . oh. He is asking me to marry him. I'm explaining that I can't leave my father."

"Why not?" Arleen asked.

"I cook all the meals, keep house, and help him run the dry goods store in town. He can't manage alone. My mother died in childbirth and my younger sister died with a fever."

"Please tell me a little more about you, Elizabeth."

"I'm twenty-five years old and my father is afraid I'm going to be an old maid," Thai answered with a little giggle. "Daddy wants me to marry Charles and be happy."

"What is happening now?"

"He has asked me several times. Now he is offering to let my father move in with us."

"Let's move forward to experience what you are going to do. On the count of three, you'll be there. One, two, three."

"I explained the offer to my father, but he declined. He insisted that I marry Charles if I loved him. I do love him. We were married in a beautiful little ceremony and now we've moved into a cabin in Cannell Meadow. Charles and a neighbor built it out of lodge pole pines. The river is half a mile away. We have a root cellar, a small barn, corrals, and a few cows and horses." Thai paused for several seconds, then said, "I'm pregnant."

"Then let's move forward to a time shortly after the baby is born," Arleen said, and provided the instructions.

"Our son is fine, and he looks like his father," Thai said proudly. "His name is Barrett."

"Is your husband still in military service?"

"Oh, no. He slipped on a rock in the river and shattered the shin bone in his right leg. They detached him from active service because of the injury."

When instructed to move forward in time to something very important that would happen in the future, Thai became very upset. "They killed him," she screamed. "The Indians killed him!"

When the regression was over, Arleen gave Thai a cassette tape of the session and explained, "I also gave you a posthypnotic suggestion to continue to remember more situations from this lifetime for the next two weeks. So, don't be surprised if you get flashes or have dreams that relate to this incarnation."

Thai waited anxiously for Michael to arrive. He didn't get off duty until 1 A.M., and it was nearly 2 A.M. before she had provided him with enough background to play the tape. As she listened to her own voice, booming larger than life, over the speakers, images began to appear and disappear in her mind . . . petroglyphs, beads, a pipe, feathers, bones, and a skull.

When the tape was over, Michael was obviously shaken by the experience. "There is absolutely no way in the world for you to know this, but you've just related a story I've heard before," he said in a choked voice. "Look at me! I have goose bumps all over my body. My great-grandmother Helen lived to be 114 years old. When I was a kid, she used to tell me stories about life in the Wyoming territory, and about Charles and Elizabeth. She would look into my eyes and call me 'Charles.' I even have one of the arrowheads taken from Charles's body when he died. We'll have to look up the details, Thai, but I don't know what to think."

Thai began to cry, not knowing why. She and Michael talked until 4:30 in the morning, then fell exhausted into bed, holding each other tightly.

"I've always loved you," she whispered.

"Me too, you," he said, softly, running his hand down her bare back and squeezing her bottom.

"M-m-m-m-m-m," she moaned. Soon they were making love with an intensity neither had experienced before. They moved from one position to another, desperately attempting to engulf each other, before relaxing into loving gentleness—barely moving, caressing, as each looked deeply into the other's eyes. Thai closed her eyes, opened them, closed them again and suddenly sat up. "What above the cave?" she said loudly.

Michael lay stunned beside her, as he attempted to figure out what was happening. He could barely see his lover in the faint illumination from the streetlight down the block. Then the words tumbled off his lips unbidden. "There was a cave near the cabin. Do you remember what was in it?"

"Yes, I do! Petroglyphs, beads, a pipe, feathers, and a skull and bones. And I just saw the cabin. I can even draw you a diagram. There was a butter churn in the corner and an old wooden bathtub."

"My parents still have the records and know a lot more than I do. I'll call them tomorrow and talk about it," Michael said, sitting up in bed beside her.

Charles Schroder McNaughton was born December 17, 1830, according to United States military records. He enlisted at the age of fifteen in Fort Sill, Oklahoma, and was promoted to sergeant in three years. A transfer was accepted February 18, 1848, to the Wyoming territory: Department of Dakota with headquarters at Fort Phil Kearny. In Wyoming, he was assigned to temporary duty in Cheyenne, where he was promoted to captain.

McNaughton married Elizabeth Michaels and the couple had a son named Barrett Daniel. Charles left active service in 1862 because of an injury but continued to serve as a scout in the northern Wyoming territory. On August 12, 1867, Captain McNaughton, Lieutenant Collins and Private Forsyth were attacked by Sioux Indians in Little Cannell Meadow. McNaughton was hit by one bullet and three arrows. He died on August 15, 1867, and was buried in an unknown location in Rendezvous Valley, now known as Jackson Hole, Wyoming.

"After discovering how accurate your regression was, I think I want to experience this for myself,"

Michael said to Thai. In his hypnotic regression session, Michael relived the birth of his son in another lifetime—more than a hundred years before. "A neighbor woman named Rosalie helped to deliver Barrett," he explained. "Her husband, Samson, helped me build the cabin."

The situation in which Michael broke his leg was traumatic. "I grazed a bear trap lying just under the water and it snapped shut, missing me, but I slipped on the rocks and fell. There was no one to help me, so I set my own leg as best I could, then waited until I was found."

In a second regression, Thai perceived additional details about the lifetime, as well as the names of others who were involved. "We're still checking these out," she said, "but before I awakened, I went forward to the last day of Elizabeth's life. She lay in bed, very tired. When she died, I watched her spirit leave through the top of her head and slowly circle the room. It was an incredible experience."

I agree with Thai when she said, "I think 123 years is long enough to wait for each other, don't you?" I asked her to add anything she could to her story. "Well, I love Michael more than I've ever loved anyone in my life. All of my adult life I've felt like I was searching without knowing what for. Now I know I've finally found it. It's really hard to explain, but I know Michael and I are soulmates and we'll be together for the rest of our lives. Three psychics have told us we'll be married within the year. I think we'll just let them be right. We're planning our wedding on a cruise ship."

16

Ellie Hildrith's Dream

"If you fear a physical activity but do it anyway, even as few as half a dozen times, a flip-flop can occur and you begin to enjoy the activity. This is called the 'opponent process theory.' In response to the act, your brain releases beta-endorphins—internally manufactured chemicals virtually identical to opium. This feels so good that you become addicted to the activity and don't want to quit," Abram Yadin, Ph.D., said.

"I don't understand how that applies to me," Ellie replied.

"Ellie Hildrith, you are a very attractive forty-year-old woman who could be enjoying your life, but you aren't. You've been coming to me once a week for almost six months; we've uncovered the cause of many fears but I have yet to convince you to go out and get involved in life. If you'll just face your fears, I'm sure you'll find they no longer exist. And even if they do, if you are willing to be afraid and act anyway, you will overcome them. To live as if your entire world revolved around your office and a television set is to waste your life." Abram waited for her to respond but she didn't.

"Ellie, if you want your life to get better, you are going to have to act. Here, let me read you something by Helen Keller. You're familiar with her story and aware of her handicaps. This is what she had to say about living: 'Security is mostly a superstition. It does not exist in nature, nor do the children of men as a whole experience it. Avoiding danger is no safer in the long run than outright exposure. Life is either a daring adventure or nothing.'"

"I see my time is up, Dr. Yadin. I'll see you next Wednesday at one." Ellie got up and carefully adjusted the belt on her skirt before reaching across the desk to shake hands with her therapist.

Outside, the downtown street was a stark contrast to the air-conditioned office. It was already too warm for a Phoenix April and the predictions were for a hotter than usual summer. She walked the two blocks down Central Avenue to the offices of Crain, Daniels and Harwood Advertising where she worked as a print media buyer.

"Any new insights?" Kay Collin asked, as Ellie walked into the cramped media area the two women shared with Rona Alden.

"Only that going without lunch every Wednesday is not enjoyable," Ellie said, smiling. "But I must subjugate my body for the sake of my mind."

"I don't think my mind is worth sixty dollars an hour," Kay replied. "Besides, spending sixty dollars a week on new clothes or makeup would do more for me mentally than any therapist."

"Maybe I'd agree with you if I had someplace to wear the makeup and clothes." Ellie's voice was distant as she put her purse in the drawer beneath her typewriter and began straightening the memos in her in-basket.

"Oh, Ellie, don't give me that. If you really wanted

to go out, I'm sure you would get plenty of offers. But you always ignore any overtures a man makes toward you, really, you do. How long has it been since you've actually had a date?"

"A couple of years, I guess. My confidence disappeared as the wrinkles appeared," she said mockingly, raising her hands to her cheeks and pulling the skin back so it lay taut against her bones.

"Ellie, you barely have any wrinkles at all! Even if you do, so what? Just date men who have more wrinkles than you do."

The door flew open with a crash. "Have you heard about Giles?" Rona blurted, entering the room at her usual breakneck pace. Dropping a stack of file folders on her desk, she turned excitedly to Ellie and Kay. "He just separated from his wife. Boy, oh boy, would I like to get together with him."

"Really? Well, how did you find that out, Rona?" Ellie asked. "Did he tell you?"

"No, his secretary did. She's been listening to the fights over the phone for months now."

"I can't believe it," Ellie said. "I wonder why his wife would ever want to leave him?"

"Probably for some of the same reasons every wife who can't get along with her husband has. And *you* certainly seem interested, Ellie, my dear," Rona purred.

"I like Giles," Ellie replied, hoping she wasn't blushing.

"Maybe you'd like to get to know him better?" Rona continued cattily.

"Rona!" Kay said sternly. "Leave Ellie alone. It's just like you to see things where they're not."

Rona nodded wisely, a sly look on her face as she left the room. "Coffee break, girls!"

"Maybe if I bleached my hair and started chewing

gum, my life would get better," Ellie said, watching Rona, her hips swinging, as she minced down the hall.

"Now don't you start meowing, too, Ellie. One Rona is more than enough! Besides, I like Giles Barton, too," Kay said. "He's certainly the nicest account exec in the company."

"Account executives are supposed to be aggressive, not nice," Ellie replied mildly.

When Ellie arrived home after work, the apartment was stuffy from being closed up all day. It was still too soon to start paying Salt River Project a large percentage of her paycheck to keep the place moderately cool when she wasn't there so it wouldn't be an oven when she was there. Ellie opened the windows and the sliding glass door leading to her small deck. After turning on her favorite FM classical station, she filled a wineglass with a California dry Chablis from the liter jug in the refrigerator.

"Not too classy, but it will do," she said aloud, relaxing into her favorite chair. The small apartment was sterile in design and decor. White walls were accented by aluminum door frames and windows, and matched by white Formica cabinets and countertops in the tiny kitchen.

"The builder must have hated wood," her father remarked, upon his first visit. Ellie had tried to compensate by decorating the apartment in Early American. The maple furnishings, bookshelves, and bric-a-brac warmed the apartment but looked out of place. "I should be looking through French doors at a countryside filled with trees being reborn in the spring showers," she often said poetically as she washed the dishes and looked out at the palm trees and the traffic on Thomas Road.

Ellie sipped the wine, her thoughts on Giles. She pushed them aside and tried to focus on other things but it didn't work. Giles' face kept reappearing before her—the way he laughed during short conversations in the office, and the media seminar they had attended together. She barely knew him but she had been enchanted the moment they were introduced. That was three years ago, when she joined the advertising agency. He was everything she had ever dreamed of in a man—but he was married. Even Dr. Yadin hadn't been able to pry these feelings out of her.

"Our daughter is going to be a classic old maid," Ellie had overheard her father once say to her mother. That was ten years ago. It had hurt but she had thought about it so many times that it didn't hurt as much any more. "Someday Ellie will find the right man," her mother had said in response. But she *hadn't* found the right man. She was too shy, too insecure, too . . . too old now. She used to date occasionally. But when the dates didn't work out, when she felt she wasn't expanding her horizons and growing, learning, she quit being interested in dating. She met no one new now. Life had become an oppressive routine and she turned to Dr. Yadin in search of a magic solution. That hadn't worked because he wasn't a magician. Not only was he not a magician, he made *her* responsible for her own pain! She snorted as she recalled the high hopes she had held that here was a man—a doctor—who would cure all her ills.

"Even if Giles gets a divorce, he wouldn't want me," she reminded herself as the visual impressions danced in and out of her mind. She was walking through a golden wheat field, holding hands with Giles. They were talking and laughing and the setting sun gleamed ruby red as he kissed her lips—sending spirals of ecstasy through her body. Passionately, she returned the kiss with mounting eagerness. He unbuttoned her blouse and she could feel the heat of his touch as his hands moved gently down the length of her back. After removing her clothing, she watched as he rolled his pants into a pillow. She moaned softly as he lay her down. He was naked, his smiling face above her. She felt her breasts crush against the hardness of his chest.

Ellie's hand was moving rapidly back and forth across her panties. "Oh, Giles," she moaned aloud with erotic pleasure as her fingers moved faster. The images intensified. She could smell the wheat field, and feel herself twisting in his arms as her body arched to meet his in a tempo that bound them together. They exploded in a downpour of fiery sensation as the sunset sky turned from magenta and orange to purple, blue, and gray before fading to black. She turned her eyes from the sky; below her lay Ellie and Giles. She was floating above them, a detached observer watching as the naked lovers now lay side by side, her head on his arm, which was gripping her tightly at the shoulder, the other arm clasping her about the waist.

But it wasn't Ellie and it wasn't Giles. It was another couple, younger, different, and they spoke in strange words she somehow understood. When the moon was high, they arose and dressed, then walked hand in hand through the fields to a dirt road. It led to a small village whose stone houses boasted uneven thatched roofs. Ellie stared wide-eyed at the carts and oxen, milk churns, and people dressed in unusual clothes.

The ringing telephone slowly pulled Ellie back to the shivering reality of a cool desert breeze blowing in off the deck across her half-naked body. She groped in the darkness for the phone. "Hi, Mom. No, no, I was in the shower and didn't hear it ringing. I'm still dripping wet. Can I call you back in a few minutes? Great. Love you, 'bye." She had been asleep for hours. The only light in the room came from the dial of the stereo receiver. Debussy's *Nocturnes,* performed by the London Symphony Orchestra, played softly in the background as she relived the dream.

The following morning, Ellie ran into Giles in the office coffee room. "I was sorry to hear about your separation from your wife."

"That's nice of you, Ellie," he replied. "But it was long overdue. There comes a time when one needs to stop fighting things that are meant to be."

"That sounds pretty metaphysical," Ellie said, smiling at him as she opened a packet of nondairy creamer to add to her coffee.

"I'm pretty metaphysical."

"Do you mean you accept psychic abilities, reincarnation, and things like that?" Ellie asked, curious.

"Yes, but don't worry, it isn't contagious," was his laughing response.

She raised her eyes to find him watching her. His whole face was smiling. "Oh, I didn't mean it like that," Ellie quickly said, apologetically. "It's just that I don't understand. I don't have any background in that sort of thing."

"If you'd like to have lunch with me, I'd be glad to explain a little more," Giles said hopefully.

"I'd love to but it's Wednesday, and on Wednesdays, I . . . well, no, that's okay. Yes, I'd like to have lunch with you and hear more about it," Ellie said. It would serve old Yadin right. He wanted her to get involved in life, didn't he? Well, she'd use his appointment time to do it.

Only during March and April does the normally sunbleached Phoenix Valley stretch greenly to the surrounding mountains. Ellie slowly twisted the stem of the Waterford crystal wineglass as she looked out the window of the rotating restaurant, twenty-eight stories above the desert floor.

"We're supposed to make a complete circle in sixty minutes," Giles said. He joined her in admiring the breathtaking view of Camelback Mountain and Scottsdale extending to the east.

"It is beautiful," Ellie said. "But I wish there were more trees. And I miss the change of the seasons."

"Me, too." The waiter delivered their drinks and Giles leaned back in his chair. Shyly, he said, "I dreamed about you the other night."

"You did? I can't believe that." She had been trying so hard to maintain her composure since he had asked her to lunch but now she could scarcely breathe. "What was I doing in the dream?"

"Nothing very exciting, I'm afraid. In fact, I'm almost embarrassed to tell you this, but you were milking a cow in an old-fashioned barn. You looked different but I knew it was you."

"Were you in it?" Ellie asked as she futilely attempted to repress a shiver that covered her arms with goose bumps.

"Yes. I was pitching hay and we were talking and laughing about something, but I don't remember what. Maybe we shared a past life."

"A past life? Do you really believe that people reincarnate?" They spent the rest of their lunch hour discussing reincarnation and were twenty minutes late getting back to the office.

"Just tell them we've been discussing media ideas," Giles said as they signed in at the reception area.

The closest metaphysical bookstore was the Alpha Book Center on East McDowell Road, only a mile or so out of Ellie's way home. "What would you suggest I read to learn more about metaphysics and reincarnation?" she asked. She left the store with *A Search for Truth* by Ruth Montgomery, *The Search for the Girl with Blue Eyes* by Jess Stearn, and *You Were Born Again to Be Together* by Dick Sutphen. "General reading on the subject," the clerk had said.

By Sunday afternoon, she had finished the three books and called the phone number in the back of one to request additional information about tapes and seminars.

Ellie planned to tell Giles about her reading program on Monday morning. She exchanged "good mornings" with Kay and listened to a not-so-brief report of her co-worker's weekend adventures. "How about you—what did you do, Ellie?" Kay asked.

"I read about reincarnation all weekend, if you can believe that," Ellie responded, knowing Kay would reprimand her for not "getting out and having fun."

"I did it, ladies," Rona announced as she entered the room, exaggeratedly swaying her hips, late as usual.

"You did what?" Kay asked.

"I got to Gilesy. He isn't bad for an older guy!" Rona smiled blissfully as she rolled her eyes.

"What do you mean, you got to Giles?" Ellie snapped.

"I mean, I let him get to me," Rona laughed, thrusting her hips forward as she sat down at her desk.

"I don't believe you," Ellie said, scowling and sitting fully erect in her chair.

"What's to believe? We were leaving at the same time Friday night and I asked him to have a drink with me. He said he didn't have anything else to do and we walked over to Enrico's. It took a while, but I got him drunk, and later, into my bed. I don't think he'd had any for a long time, the way he went for it."

"You're disgusting," Ellie said in a loud voice, throwing a copy of *Standard Rates & Data* on the floor as she got up hastily to walk out of the room.

"What difference does it make to you?" Rona asked. "Besides, he's leaving anyway."

Ellie was almost to the doorway when she turned around. "What do you mean Giles is leaving?" Her voice almost broke on the last word.

"Well, well, well. I think Miss Priss has a crush on ol' Giles, don't you, Kay?" Kay didn't respond and Rona continued. "He's resigned. Giles has given his notice and is moving back to wherever he came from. Connecticut, I think."

Stiffly, Ellie turned and left. In the coffee room, she held on to the sink, trying to catch her breath. "Get hold of yourself, Ellie. This is absolutely ridiculous," she told herself. "You are nothing to Giles but one of the girls in the office. He's been nice to you just like he is to everyone else. He isn't interested in you—he could easily find someone prettier and a hell of a lot more fun. Like Rona . . . Rona . . . RONA!!!"

"Ellie, are you all right?" She jumped. It was Giles. He put his hand gently on her shoulder. She hadn't noticed him entering the room.

"How could you, with that tramp?" Ellie yelled. "I know you don't owe me anything! I just . . . don't believe . . . it's just that you're so special. Ah, forget it! I have no right to . . ." Her words trailed off and she turned and ran down the hall. In seconds, she had grabbed her purse and was making her way toward the safety of the stairs. No one followed her and soon she was behind the wheel of her Honda, driving east on Thomas Road.

You little idiot! The moment you begin to get involved in life, you blow it, Ellie. You made a fool of yourself! Now you can never *go back,* she thought despairingly, tears blurring her vision.

The office buildings on the palm tree lined street became apartments, then residences, as she approached the suburbs. "God, I hate palm trees! And I hate the heat! And I hate all the plastic-looking buildings! Oh, but you belong here, Ellie," she whispered viciously to herself, her knuckles white as she gripped the steering wheel. "You belong in a city that has no real heritage, no soul, because *you* have no soul. You're just a pretend person living in a pretend city with pretend trees."

The Honda screeched to a halt in front of her apartment. Blankly, she contemplated her front door then shook her head. "I've got to get out of here, got to get away," she whispered, her throat raw with tears.

The phone was ringing when she opened her apartment door but she didn't answer it. It kept ringing as she quickly packed a suitcase, and it was still ringing when she slammed the door behind her. She fled to the mountains, staying in a little town called Payson, seventy miles above the Phoenix Valley. She spent four days in a motel on the edge of town, but most of the time, she sat beside a creek behind the motel. "I'm sure I don't have a job any more, so now what am I going to do with the rest of my life?"

It was hard to keep her thoughts focused. A floating leaf would grasp her attention, pulling her mind along with the current, over the rocks and down the creek. Tall pines lined the far bank, the edge of a forest leading north to the White Mountains and the Apache Indian reservation.

Ellie didn't find any answers but she did come to the conclusion that life wasn't any worse than it had been before she allowed herself to think seriously about Giles. He was still very much in her thoughts, but she had resigned herself to his presence and stopped fighting it.

She was welcomed home by the blinking light of her answering machine in the darkness. It indicated numerous calls which she had no desire to know about. She had called her parents from Payson and the rest of the world could go to hell. It was now ten o'clock on Thursday evening.

Ellie sat with a glass of wine, shuffling distractedly through the pile of mail. One piece caught her eye— *Master of Life* magazine. Oh, yes, it was in response to her call for more information about reincarnation. She opened it curiously. Inside were stories about karma, dharma, and how to develop psychic ability. In the seminar section was a lengthy description of a seminar taking place that very weekend in Santa Monica, California.

"Why not? I'm certainly not ready to face anyone around here," she said to herself as she poured another glass of wine.

Ellie registered for the seminar by phone Friday morning and spent the rest of the day driving to Los Angeles. It was a nine-hour trip on Interstate 10, crossing a desert already reaching one hundred degrees by mid-morning. Nine hours of thinking about Giles. About the dream he had and of her own dream as she masturbated. Or was that afterward? It didn't matter, did it? She hadn't masturbated since, fearing it would happen again, causing her to long for a man she couldn't have—a man who was moving back East in a few days. A man she would never see again.

When she walked into the seminar room, the people surprised her. Their ages ranged from around thirty to at least seventy, she decided, and they were as normal-looking a group as her fellow employees in the advertising agency. "Ex-fellow employees," she mentally corrected.

The activities began with an exploration of karma. "The unerring law of karma is always adjusting and balancing as a result of your free choices. And every condition in your current life is karmic in nature . . . karma that you have generated up to this very moment." The more Ellie heard, the more she identified with the logic of it all.

The rest of the morning consisted of preparation exercises for hypnosis and past-life regression. After lunch, the lights of the hotel ballroom were dimmed and the 150 participants were told they could experience the regression either sitting in their chairs or lying on the carpeted floor. Ellie chose to lie down, using her jacket for a pillow. She responded easily to the body relaxation and felt her body, part by part, slowly fading into the background.

During the countdown, she visualized herself running down a hill in a beautiful wooded countryside. Far away, a distant voice was saying, "I want your superconscious mind to choose a lifetime that would be of value for you to explore at this time." She tried to hold on to the reality of the voice and the room, but she no longer felt her body at all, and the early morning sunshine on her face was so much more appealing. Breathing the crisp mountain air deeply, she untied the rope which fastened the pasture gate securely, and put a halter on the waiting cow. "Come along, Joletta," she said, laughing as she walked down the path toward the barn. Inside, the sun streamed brightly through the spaces between the boards as she coaxed the cow's head into the milking stall. And then Giles was there. He was young, his blond hair shining as he walked up and kissed her on the nose. She laughed and kissed him on the mouth, and then he was gone, exiting through a side door, carrying a rake.

"Let go of this now," said the faraway voice. "I want you to remember everything you are perceiving, but let go of this and move on to another situation. I want you to move through time to something very important that is about to happen in your future. On the count of three, vivid impressions will begin to come in. One, two, three."

"Oh-h-h-h-h-h!" It was her own voice crying out in the blackness. When she opened her eyes, she was on her back with her legs raised; beyond her stood two women dressed in layered clothes and bonnets. "It's a girl. You have a fine bitty girl, Tourmaline," said one of the women. "I'll tell Jardine," said the other, leaving the room. Moments later, she was holding her baby and she felt the joyful tears on her cheeks. Giles was there, smiling and talking . . . but he wasn't Giles, he was Jardine, and he was telling her over and over how much he loved her and that it was all right, they would have a boy next time. "I want to name her Monette," she said softly.

"And now let go of this," the distant voice interrupted again. "Remember every detail of what you are perceiving, but I want you to let go of this and move through time to another very important situation involving you and the most important person to you in this lifetime we are now exploring. On the count of three, vivid impressions will begin to come in. One, two, three."

They were walking on the ice. Monette was now five or six and she was chasing Jardine, throwing snowballs and laughing, when the ice suddenly cracked and gave way beneath them . . . and they were gone. "Noooooo!"

Ellie used the self-release suggestion she had been given, raising her right hand a little and counting from one to five. She sat up in the dim light of the hotel ballroom. Around her were what seemed to be sleeping people. In response to the hypnotic suggestion, she had awakened "calm and at peace with the world and everyone in it," but she remembered everything, and in remembering, she couldn't help but feel drained.

After everyone was awake and alert, the participants were asked to share what they had experienced in the past-life regression. Those who volunteered were given a microphone. The first woman was in her fifties, dressed in California beach attire, and her voice cracked as she attempted to hold back tears. "I was in Europe, probably in the Middle Ages, and my husband and I belonged to a group of people that traveled from village to village, selling goat's milk and fixing things. Gypsies, I suppose. I saw myself working on a copper pot. There were about seven or eight of us; my husband seemed to be our leader. But then some townspeople came in the night and accused us of stealing. It was terrible what they did to him. Terrible! Then they crushed our hands—crushed them so we could not milk the goats or do our work. I don't know what happened to us . . . we probably starved to death.

"Look," she said, holding up a gloved hand. "All my life I've worn gloves, not because I think they're fashionable—I've worn them for protection. In this life, I've always been overly protective of my hands."

A young man in his mid-thirties, dressed in jeans and a sweater, was the next to share. "I've always loved horses," he said. "And now I think I know why. My regression was in Montana, in the mid-1800s. I was a ranchhand. It was my responsibility to take care of the horses, I guess because I was small and not especially strong. But I doctored the horses and even slept in a small room near the stables. When you asked about the most important person in my life, I saw myself talking with the wife of the man who owned the ranch. She was older and took a liking to me. She'd slip me a fresh loaf of bread and say, 'I've got to fatten you up, Freddy.' "

Several others shared their stories, all showing patterns of cause and effect. After a brief break, the next group regression was a "Back To The Cause Karmic Cleansing" session. The participants were told to choose a situation in their lives they would like to better understand—it could be a fear, a problem, a phobia, or a relationship situation. The goal of the regression was to be summarized in one sentence. Ellie worded her suggestion, "I want to know the reason I am so reluctant to get involved with others and enjoy my life."

Lying once again on the floor, her body relaxed even more rapidly than it had the first time she listened to the suggestions. She was running down the same hill; from far away the voice was saying, "Number five, deeper, deeper, deeper, down, down, down. Number four, deeper, deeper . . ." The numbers and suggestions faded in and out of reality as she ran faster and faster down the hill, down the hill, down the hill. "On the next count, vivid impressions will begin to come in, impressions of an event that is responsible for your current reality. N-u-m-b-e-r o-n-e."

They were walking on the ice. Monette was now five or six and she was chasing Jardine, throwing snow-balls and laughing, until the ice gave way and they were gone. "NOOOOOO . . ." She ran screaming to the open hole but stopped as the ice began to crack underfoot. "JARDINE, MONETTE, OH, LORD, NO, NO, NOOOOOOOO."

"There was nothing anyone could have done," they told her. "A hundred strong men couldn't have saved them once they slipped under the ice in that freezing water. It was God's will," they said. "You must pick up your life and start over again," they advised.

"START OVER AGAIN?" she screamed. "Start over again? I will never, ever allow myself to feel anything for anybody. Why should I, when a vengeful God only takes them away to make you suffer! Well, he can't make me suffer if I don't care, can he?"

And from far away, the voice was saying, "It is time to let go of this and come back to the present. You will remember everything you are experiencing, but on the count of three, you will be back in the present and you will become aware of how the people in your past relate to your present. One, two, three."

Ellie watched the images in her mind; the faces of Giles and Jardine overlapped and became one. And there were Monette and Ellie's mother—they also merged and then faded away. And there was only darkness, and a quietness of spirit that penetrated her body and mind.

"All right. Now, on the count of three, I want you to perceive very strong impressions about how to rise above this karma," the voice boomed over the sound system. "Is it already nearly balanced? Have you almost learned so that you can let go of the effect? What can you do to rise above this karma? It will amount to *self-forgiveness*, but to truly forgive yourself, you must know on every level of your body and mind that you will never, ever forget the lesson again. So, if you are not yet able to forgive yourself to that degree, what can you do to cleanse yourself . . . to forgive yourself? Is there some form of symbolic restitution that will help you to prove to yourself that you have learned the desired karmic lesson? Let the impressions come in now. One, two, three."

Nothing appeared, no pictures, no voices,

nothing. Ellie began to grow impatient but decided to think about the situation. "If karma is reality, then what happened in the past was to resolve things that had happened in even earlier times. My present reality seems to be a direct result of vows I made to avoid feeling anything for anybody. The reason I did that was to avoid pain, but I've only carried it forward into this life. Just because I lost those I most loved doesn't mean I will again." She recalled Dr. Yadin's words, "Ellie, if you insist on living with one foot in the safety zone, you will never experience your potential for a joyful life."

Her thoughts were interrupted by a vivid impression of Giles and an inner voice saying, "Act . . . act . . . act . . ."

It was late Monday afternoon before she was home in Phoenix. The tape on the answering machine had nearly run out. She rewound it and pushed the "play" button. There was a call from Kay; she wanted to come over and talk. Her parents had called, and they, too, were concerned. And then Giles' voice came on, saying, "Ellie, this is Giles. I would really like to talk to you. Maybe we can get together for dinner. I'll call later, please answer the phone. Good-bye." There were several hang-up clicks, and then Giles again, this time leaving his phone number. "Please call me, Ellie. I'm worried about you—it's been two days. I really care."

As Ellie listened to the eighth phone call from Giles, the dam inside her broke and the hot, scalding tears flooded her face. She brought her hands to her face and sobbed as she listened. "Ellie, it's Sunday night and I'm desperate. You're all I can think about. I don't think you have any idea how much I've cared about you since I first met you, but you were always so distant, so elusive. It wasn't until you confronted me in the office that I had any indication that you shared my feelings. I should have spoken up long ago but you probably don't realize how shy I really am. I'm nearly sixty years old and here I am proposing to an answering machine . . . but I love you and there is nothing I'd like more than to have you say you'll come to Connecticut with me. Oh, Ellie, please, please call me, my dearest." His voice broke, then she heard the click as he hung up. The rest of the tape was blank.

It was several months after Ellie attended my Santa Monica seminar that she sent me a letter explaining her story. The following is the last paragraph of that letter:

"Giles and I were married in September. We have a wonderful life and a beautiful home on three acres of the most incredibly gorgeous wooded countryside. As I write this, I am looking out the French doors of our dining room, watching Giles as he rakes the falling leaves together. He is calling for me to come and help. Thanks again so very, very much for your part in my transformation. Much love, Ellie."

CHAPTER

17

Some Clarifying Questions and Answers

Q. The concept of reincarnation is so silly. How can an intelligent person accept it?

A. If an intelligent person is going to accept any spiritual concept, how could he accept anything else? That's a better question. Reincarnation and karma is the only religion/philosophy that can logically explain all the injustice and inequality in the world. And rather than being at odds with science, as is every other spiritual system, metaphysics/reincarnation correlates perfectly with scientific awareness.

Science teaches that the universe operates on a principal of vibrational energy. Einstein discovered that matter is energy. Matter appears solid but is, in reality, pulsating molecules of energy. The chair you are sitting on is composed of zillions of pulsating molecules. Your skin is composed of swiftly moving molecules orbiting each other with great exchanges of energy. These molecules are vibrating at a specific rate, forming matter.

Science also teaches that energy can't die—it can only transform. To prove this, physicists have isolated the smallest molecule of energy within a sealed cloud chamber. Nothing else can get in and the molecule can't get out. Although too small to see with the naked eye, the molecule can be photographed on ultra-high-speed sensitive film.

The film shows that the molecule has a size, a weight, a pattern, and a speed. And it exists within the cloud chamber until it falls to the bottom, appearing to die. But it doesn't die. The scientists leave the camera running, and pretty soon, the molecule is back. It has transformed—it has a new size, a new weight, a new pattern, and a new speed. And this goes on indefinitely.

You are energy. Your body is energy. Your mind is energy. Your soul is energy. And the only difference between a chair and a plant and your body, mind, and soul is their vibrational rate. You can't die—you can only transform, which is another way to say reincarnate.

So, how does all this work with metaphysics? Perfectly! Metaphysics teaches that you were born into this life with a soul level vibrational rate you earned as a result of how you lived your past lives (as discussed in the Rob Bradwick chapter). You are here on the earth to raise your vibrational rate by letting go of fear and expressing unconditional love.

Why do you want to raise your vibrational rate? Maybe it is because you want to progress to the God-head level. Or, it could be the only way to end your cycles of reincarnations. That's a pretty good reason. Or, since everything on the earth is vibrational energy, you are part of a large energy gestalt. Maybe by raising your own vibrational rate, you do your part to create additional energy for the gestalt. Science teaches that energy can't stand still. It must, by its very nature, move forward or backward. To stand still is to stagnate and since we don't want to stagnate, we each do our part to move the energy forward.

Within your Higher Self is what Carl Jung calls the "collective unconscious." Metaphysics teaches that we are all one, and since we are all part of the collective unconscious, this is correct. We are all connected on this level—part of the gestalt—the whole. Personally, I like to call the gestalt "God" but any other name would serve as well.

Q. How does metaphysics correlate with the scientific theory that a resonant field is established by cumulative experience, making it is easier to learn something new if it has already been learned by others?

A. Again metaphysics and science network perfectly. Go back to the idea of the collective unconscious—the level of supreme enlightenment. Although most of us are not yet able to retain contact with this level of our totality, we can be influenced if we are open. The more people that learn something new, the larger the volume of awareness on the new subject in the collective awareness of mankind.

This concept also explains why different people come up with simultaneous discoveries. Mankind as a group has attained the prerequisite knowledge for the birth of the new idea. So it is there, just waiting, and those most attuned may discover it at the same time, as history has often recorded.

Q. Please capsulize the concept of karma.

A. Karma means balance and the supreme potential of balance is harmony. We are all here on earth to attain harmony. According to Newtonian physics, "for each and every action, there is an equal and opposite

218

reaction." In Biblical terms that translates to "as you sow, so shall you reap." In today's slang it is "what goes around comes around." I personally prefer "cause and effect."

Through cause and effect, we eventually learn what creates disharmony and what creates harmony. Every choice we make is creating our future. There is a metaphysical axiom that says, "You are what you think, having become what you thought." Cause and effect begins with your thoughts, which are then expressed as spoken words and actions.

All karma is self-imposed testing to see if you have learned to respond to life harmoniously. *Reward Karma* is your accumulation of positive earthly potential, such as good health, career success, a counterpart soulmate, or good family relationships. Suppose you've earned the karmic right to easy wealth and fame. This is also an important test of responsibility. Do you use the money and position selfishly or do you use it as an opportunity to assist others? How you handle your fame and fortune will be the deciding factor in allowing yourself to retain what you have gained, in this life or in future lives.

Or, reward karma could simply be viewed as the right to be born under more ideal astrological influences. We are all walking examples of our astrological birth times. While one set of planetary combinations may generate a mellow, self-confident personality, another combination may result in a hyperactive or self-destructive personality. Although all planetary configurations have both positive and negative aspects, some are more easily overcome than others.

Self-Punishment Karma is to balance past disharmonious actions. The quickest way is to directly experience the consequences of your actions. As an example, let's say you find yourself in a situation of extreme poverty to balance a past life in which you totally misused wealth. This is self-punishment. It is also self-testing, for your life is so miserable that it would be easy to turn to crime or commit suicide. The test is to live through it properly. Since wisdom erases karma this could also release you from your poverty within your current life.

THE 5 CATEGORIES OF KARMA

There are five categories of karma which can fall either under self-reward or self-punishment.

BALANCING KARMA

This is the most simplistic, mechanical kind of cause and effect. Examples of balancing karma would be a lonely man who seeks unsuccessfully to establish a relationship. In a past life, he used others so cruelly that he needs to learn the value of a relationship.

Other examples: A man who is always overlooked for promotion because in a past life he destroyed others to attain wealth and power; a woman who suffers continual, severe migraine headaches because, in a fit of jealousy, she hit her lover on the head and killed him in a past life; a man who is born blind because, as a Roman soldier, he purposely blinded Christian prisoners.

PHYSICAL KARMA

Physical karma is a situation in which a past-life problem or misuse of the body results in an appropriate affliction in a later life. Physical karma usually results from reincarnating too soon—before the etheric body has reformed, as in the Randi Mabrey chapter.

As an example, a child born with lung problems might relate back to excessive smoking and death from lung cancer in a past life. Another man with a disfiguring birthmark found it to be a carry-over from a terrible burn in a past life.

FALSE-FEAR KARMA

False-fear karma is created when a traumatic past-life incident generates a fear that is not valid in the context of the current life.

For example, a workaholic finds out in regression that he could not feed his family during a time of famine in the Middle Ages. He reexperiences the pain of burying a child who starved to death. In his current life, his subconscious mind is attempting to avert any potential duplication of that terrible pain, thus generating an internal drive to work day and night to assure adequate provision for his family in this incarnation.

False-fear karma and false-guilt karma are the easiest to resolve through past-life therapy techniques because once the individuals understand the origin of the fear and/or guilt, they can see how it no longer applies to them in their current lifetime.

FALSE-GUILT KARMA

False-guilt karma occurs when an individual takes on the responsibility or accepts the blame for a traumatic past-life incident for which he or she is blameless from any perspective.

A man who contracted polio resulting in a paralyzed leg perceived as the past-life cause his being the driver of a car which was involved in an accident that crippled a child. Although it wasn't his fault, he blamed himself and sought self-forgiveness through this karmic affliction.

Situations involving depression and/or emotional problems can almost always be traced to a tragedy of some kind in which guilt is associated with the event. This can be false guilt or a situation in which the troubled individual was actually responsible for the tragedy. The Debra Wakefield chapter demonstrates the disharmonious power of false guilt.

DEVELOPED ABILITY AND AWARENESS KARMA

Abilities and awareness are developed over a period of many lifetimes.

As examples, a man in Rome became interested in music and began to develop his ability. Today, after six additional lifetimes in which he became a little better with each life, he is a successful professional musician. A woman happily married for thirty-five years has worked hard to refine her awareness of human relationships over many lifetimes.

The abilities and awareness that you master over a period of lifetimes are yours to keep forever, although they may lie latent, buried deep within you, waiting for a time when it is appropriate to call them into your present existence.

Q. Exactly what is the Higher Self?

A. When you attain a Higher-Self level of consciousness, you have an awareness of your totality. You have an understanding of your past lives and the present as it relates to you or anyone else you care to psychically know. How can this be? Because you are accessing the totality—the energy gestalt called "God." In other words, your Higher Self is the collective awareness of the gestalt. It is The All That Is . . . The Oneness.

So, is *your* Higher Self the same as *my* Higher

Self? Of course. We are both part of the same gestalt—part of God. People argue that their Higher Self is a separate entity. This might be accurate if viewed as a superior intelligence/awareness but it's a limiting perspective. Your Higher Self isn't your spirit guide or a Master teacher; it is the awareness of all that has ever been, all that is, and all that can potentially be.

Q. If we predestine some painful experiences, then we don't really have free will in these areas, do we?

A. Although you may have predestined some painful events, *wisdom erases karma.* The balancing of karma is *to teach, not punish.* Once you have truly learned your lesson and know on a soul level you will never make the karmic mistake again, you'll forgive yourself—experiencing no more pain in this area of your life. You are your own judge and jury, so your fate is completely in your hands. But your soul is totally moral. You can't lightly say, "Oh, I've learned that was wrong, so I forgive myself," and expect to eliminate painful karma.

In my *Karmic Cleansing Regression* seminars, the hypnotized group is directed to the cause. After allowing time for them to reexperience events from their past (in this life or a past life), I say, "On the count of three, I want you to perceive impressions about how to rise above this karma. Is it already nearly balanced? Have you almost learned so that you can let go of the effect? If you are not yet ready to forgive yourself what can you do to accelerate the process? Is there some form of symbolic restitution which will assist you to attain balance?"

An example: A female participant could not have children. Medical tests revealed nothing wrong with her or her husband. But in regression she relived a lifetime in which she abandoned a child. Until she learns on a soul level about the value of life and the responsibility of children, she will block herself from having a child. Today, as symbolic restitution, she does part-time volunteer work in a hospital for crippled children. Hopefully, her work will help her achieve self-forgiveness.

Also, as Edgar Cayce said, "The law of grace supersedes the law of karma." If you give love and mercy, you'll receive the same in return. A painful predestined event can be mitigated by how you live your life from the time you are born until the time of the event. Or, from this moment up to the time of the event. The more positive, loving and compassionate you are, the more you may modify the experience. And the more enlightened you are, the less meaning any event will have.

There is another aspect of free will that is extremely important: Although an event may be predestined, your reaction to the event allows total free will. If you respond with positive emotions, you've obviously learned your lessons and won't need to be tested again. If you respond with negativity, anger, hatred, resentment, or hostility, you'll have to go through it again and again until you resolve the fear.

CHAPTER

18

The 13 Channels of Awareness

For ten years, twice a year, I've taught a weeklong seminar called Past-Life Therapy Techniques. The participants come from all over the world to learn to hypnotize, and to incorporate metaphysical awareness into their existing holistic/psychic career, or as a step toward establishing a practice. Some of those in attendance plan to incorporate the awareness into careers as human-potential trainers or New Age seminar leaders.

This professional training covers many areas of expertise, yet basic to all the awareness is what I call the *Critical 13*. When someone explains his problem to a counselor or stands up in a seminar room to talk about his problem, *the cause of his turmoil will always be one or more of these 13 factors.* So, the counselor, therapist or trainer must learn to listen for these factors in the dialogue with his subject. Usually one or more will quickly become obvious. Upon this recognition, the therapist/trainer begins verbal "processing," by asking the right questions; the subject's answers indicate the next step in the processing. The professional chooses one of seven approaches for this verbal interrogation: 1. Support, 2. Shock, 3. A Weaving Into Awareness, 4. Attack/Insult, 5. Tease, 6. Appear to Sympathize/Agree, 7. Irritate/Anger.

Once the therapist/trainer understands the problem, he will use "Back To The Cause" hypnotic regression techniques when there appears to be no known cause. The therapist/trainer's goal is always to assist his subject to let go of fear and to learn to express unconditional love.

The following information is provided to use as a basis for self-processing. Then, if your problem appears to be rooted in a past life, you may want to work with a professional past-life therapist. Or you may choose to regress yourself with self-hypnosis or use prerecorded past-life regression tapes to find the cause of your present effects. After discussing each of the 13 factors I will provide the general "action required" to rise above the negativity, and a representative dialogue from my *Master of Life Seminars*.

1. BELIEFS

A belief is something you don't know. If it is a negative belief it's obviously fear. But positive beliefs can also be based upon fear. You believe your country is the greatest in the world, for to believe otherwise is fearful. You believe in God because not to believe in God is fearful. You believe your mate is faithful. You believe you can count on your friends. You believe your job is secure.

You are served by many of your positive beliefs, but it is important to realize if they are based on fear. If a problem relates to a belief, the *action required* is an examination of the belief in relationship to reality. The belief needs to be tested against *"what is."* I'll be talking more about what is as we proceed.

Beliefs generate your thoughts and emotions which create all your experiences. You create your own reality with your beliefs, which often relate back to past-life experiences. It is important to realize your beliefs are not buried deep in your subconscious mind. They are part of your conscious awareness. It is just that they go unexamined because you accept them as *facts.*

Beliefs are the basis of everything in your life. Sure, it's easy to recognize your religious and political beliefs, but I'm talking about your core beliefs—who and what you are: your success, weight, health, relationships or lack of relationships, career, and everything else central to your existence.

As examples: You believe you can only be so successful, so that's as successful as you are. You believe your body is fat, so you are. If you change your belief, you change your subconscious programming and your body weight aligns with the new programming. Hypnosis tapes, subliminals and sleep programming tapes, which are so popular today, do only one thing. They change your old beliefs by programming new beliefs into your subconscious mind.

Self-processing of resentments related to your beliefs can also be valuable. A Universal law says *you cannot become what you resent.* This law is absolute because *you always live up to your self-image.* As an example, let's say you are overweight and when you see someone with a beautiful body, you make a snide comment such as, "All beauty and no brains." In so doing you doom yourself to being overweight because if people with beautiful bodies have no brains, you will never allow yourself to have a beautiful body. You certainly don't want to be brainless.

As another example, let's say you are actively seeking monetary success, but at a stoplight, when you pull up beside a Rolls-Royce, you look over and think, "Rich people are such snobs." Again, you are assuring you will never be rich. You wouldn't allow yourself to live up to a self-image of a snob.

Adelle: Seminar Dialogue

Adelle, a dark-haired beauty in her early thirties, raised her hand to request a microphone. "It isn't logical, but I realized in the group belief process that my belief about marriage is, 'All the good men are already taken, so don't bother.' "

"What is your experience in regard to the belief?" I asked.

"Well, I guess I think this. But I have lots of dates, and actually, many of the men are great. However, I never let them get very serious," she replied, flashing an amused grin.

"Would you like to get married if you found the right man?"

"Yes, consciously I would. But you've got me concerned about my subconscious programming." She shrugged matter-of-factly. "I'd hate to be fooling myself for the next twenty years."

Seminar participants are taught a technique for instant hypnosis. This allows me to quickly regress individuals during the processing sessions. Adelle wanted to explore the cause of her belief, so I directed the induction process and told her, "You may go back to an earlier time in your present life, or you may return to an event that transpired in a previous incarnation. On the count of three, you'll experience vivid impressions relating to the cause of your belief about men and marriage. One, two, three."

"There's a woman . . . she's crying." Her voice was soft and low.

"Are you the woman?" I asked.

"I think so. She's about to be married, but she isn't very happy about it."

"I want you to attain a complete understanding of the situation. You have the power and ability to do this. Move forward in time if necessary. When you have the awareness, speak up and share it with me."

Adelle was silent, her eyes darting back and forth beneath her eyelids. "My father says I should be married. My sisters are all married, my friends are married. He's afraid I'm going to be an old maid, so I am marrying Reece. I don't love him, but no one else is interested in me—I have no choice."

After exploring additional details of this Welsh lifetime, I directed Adelle to let go of the past-life impressions and ascend into her Higher Self. "All right, Adelle, I want you to talk to me about how this relates to your present life."

"Obviously, my belief has been programmed by a fear of repeating a painful past-life experience. It's a false fear that will imprison me until I confront it. If I am open to loving and being loved, I can transcend the programming."

Most of the following factors are actually beliefs rooted in self-deception, but for the sake of rapid communication there is often value in approaching them from other perspectives.

2. ASSUMED LIMITATIONS AND FAULTY ASSUMPTIONS

These factors are active in all our lives to some degree. Here are some examples: "I'm a $25,000 a year commissioned sales rep, but I'm not capable of being a $75,000 a year man." "If I'm direct and honest in my communications, I'll probably lose all my friends." "I'd really love to have a good relationship, but it isn't possible being married to Fred."

Usually, assumed limitations and faulty assumptions are directly related to your self-image and the size of your vision. Until you become aware of your mental limitations, it is unlikely you'll do anything to rise above them.

Action required: Realize the limitations and assumptions are self-imposed beliefs. They are not real. The next step to rise above the effects of restrictive thinking is to become clear on your intent. Exactly what do you want, why do you want it, and what are you willing to do to get it?

Mark: Seminar Dialogue

"I don't think it is a faulty assumption to realistically appraise your limitations," Mark said, challenge in his voice. He was in his mid-thirties and wore a casual suit.

"Apply this to your life, Mark. What are you talking about?" I asked, leaving the stage to move closer to him.

"I'd like to marry a beautiful woman, but I'm neither handsome nor successful enough to attract one."

"What does love have to do with beauty?" I asked.

"I didn't say anything about love," he snapped.

"Oh, you just want to marry her as a showpiece?"

"Well, ah, no. It's just that it would make me feel good if she was beautiful."

"What if she was a stark-raving, beautiful bitch?"

He shrugged his shoulders and tilted his head to one side, in reply. "What's really going on with you, Mark? This has nothing to do with beautiful women."

"I don't know what you mean."

"Yes, you do. Who would be impressed by your beautiful wife?"

Mark's eyes narrowed and he gave me a hard, cynical smile. "Everybody!"

"Everybody, huh? What would they think about you because you had a beautiful wife?"

He hesitated momentarily, then blurted, "That I must really be something special to get her!"

"That's a faulty assumption, Mark. You're attempting to bolster your self-image externally, which will never work. We all have a basic psychological need to feel worthwhile to ourselves and others. But self-image results from what we do in life, not from what we have. Also—and this is critical—you must maintain a satisfactory standard of behavior and correct yourself when you're wrong. When your conduct is below your standard and you don't correct it, your self-image will suffer."

"Well, that's a lot easier said than done," Mark responded impatiently.

"Mark, psychiatry is concerned with two basic psychological needs. The need to love and be loved, and the need to feel worthwhile. You need to begin building self-esteem by examining your behavior. Wise choices between realistic and unrealistic behavior is simply what we call reason. Tell me what you do that makes you feel good about yourself."

He hesitated, looked at the floor, crossing and uncrossing his arms. "Ah, well. I'd like to go to night school and learn about computers so I can get a better job. But I haven't had the time."

"You've just been 'way too busy,' huh?" I said in a sympathetic tone.

"Yes." He realized I was mocking him and scowled. "Well, maybe the reason I'm not all that responsible is karma?"

"Everything is karma, so I'm sure it is. But wisdom erases karma, Mark. If you were regularly visiting one of the new breed of psychotherapists, he would work to get you to be more responsible and realistic about making immediate sacrifices to attain long-term satisfaction."

"I can't afford therapy," he said.

"Then I'll give you the bottom line and it will be up to you to act on it. 1. Decide what you are doing that isn't working. 2. Make immediate changes in your behavior. They will quickly lead to a change in attitude, which will lead to the fulfillment of your need to feel worthwhile. It's that simple, but that doesn't necessarily mean easy."

"Thank you," he said, sitting down.

3. BLAMING AND VICTIMS

It is easier to be a victim and blame others for your circumstances than it is to take responsibility for your life. From a metaphysical perspective, blame is totally incompatible with reincarnation and karma. We are here on earth to learn, and we set up the circumstances as tests to judge our level of awareness. Since you assigned yourself your lessons, there is no one but yourself to blame for anything.

So, think about all the people who have victimized you: your mate who divorced you, your friend who betrayed you, your business partner who ripped you off. You can't blame them. They supplied the opportunities you needed to experience. Thank them. Release them.

From a human-potential perspective, blame is self-pity. Relate this to your life and you'll realize how true it is. Plus, self-pity is negative programming of your subconscious mind, so it is doubly destructive.

Action required: Realize the futility of blame. You are the only one harmed by the illusion. The acceptance of self-actualized metaphysical philosophy will transform the way you experience the negativity.

Nicole: Seminar Dialogue

"My husband ran off with my best friend, leaving me with three kids," Nicole said, one hand on her hip in an assertive stance. Her tone was cool disapproval. "And you're telling me not to blame?"

"But, that's what you wanted him to do, Nicole," I replied, toying with her.

"You're crazy," said, shaking the microphone at me.

"Want to explore it in regression?"

"Sure," she said tersely.

Nicole went quickly into a deep, altered state of consciousness. I directed her back to the cause of her marital breakup. "Speak up and tell me what you perceive."

"Fire! There's fire. My boat's on fire. Curjew! Tell the men, Maggot." Nicole's voice was agitated and she was trembling.

"What's happening now?"

"Leavin' . . . before I burn my arse. Rowin' into the dark."

"Are your men with you in the boat?"

"Nah."

"Are they still on the burning boat?"

"Yeah."

"Are there more small boats for them?"

"Nah."

"You said, 'my boat.' Are you the captain?"

"So what?"

"Did you abandon your men, Captain?"

"So what. They're just scum."

From Higher Self, I asked Nicole to talk to me about how the past life related to her present situation.

"Eighteen men died in the boat fire. I am beginning to resolve my karma by learning what it means to be abandoned. My present bitterness about Jack leaving shows I've learned nothing. Unless I can forgive him for leaving and myself for what I did, I will continue to experience similar situations in this life and future lives. Blithe, my best friend who ran off with Jack, was one of the men on the ship."

4. NEGATIVE PAYOFF

A negative payoff is a situation in which you say you want something to be different than it is, but consciously or subconsciously, you block the desired goal because there is a payoff in maintaining the status quo. A good example of this was a woman in a seminar who said she desired to be wealthy. She worked hard and used programming techniques to support her goals. Yet, when I began to process her, it became obvious she was subconsciously blocking her own success out of love for her father. If she allowed herself to "show him up," he would be hurt and she would experience the guilt.

In another case a woman claimed she wanted to find a husband. But she was extremely overweight and did nothing to make herself more attractive. During processing, she said a mate would be possessive—restricting her activities and complicating her life. "I'm not too fond of fixing meals on schedule, or washing and ironing either," she added. Obviously, no matter how much she talks about wanting to get married, there is a bigger payoff in remaining single.

Action required: Explore your goals and desires. Ask yourself, 1. "If I get what I want, what will change?" 2. "What are the potential undesirable changes?" The negative payoffs will be in number two.

Hollis: Seminar Dialogue

Hollis raised his hand for the microphone, and when he received it, stood looking at the floor for a while as if to build anticipation. He was dressed in a cotton sport coat, a T-shirt, and jeans. "I'm trying to see the negative payoff in my failed business ventures," he finally said.

"Tell me about them, Hollis."

"Oh, I've tried so many things, but they never work. Car washes, hamburger stands . . . you name it."

"What do you really find joy in doing?"

"Writing. I'm a free-lance writer and I love it. It's just that it doesn't pay well enough. I have to find a way to make more money," he said solemnly.

"You're a good writer? You do it naturally and well? It's fun?"

"Absolutely!"

"If your other businesses were to succeed, would they reduce or eliminate your writing time?"

"Yes, but . . . oh shit!" A flash of understanding shot across Hollis's face.

"You don't dare let yourself succeed then, do you?" He slowly nodded his head in agreement. "Why

235

not focus your energy on finding new ways to make money writing, instead of assuming a limitation?"

He flashed a thumbs up signal as he sat down.

5. MASKS OR ACTS

There are three ways to generate change in a human being. 1. Add something to their life: people, things, environment, awareness, programming, challenge, etc. 2. Subtract something from their life: people, things, environment, challenge, etc. 3. Get the person to be himself. This is transcendental change. Accepting what is in yourself is the beginning of transformation, because you can't change what you don't recognize.

When you wear masks you are attempting to avoid pain. You think the real you isn't adequate enough, or impressive enough, or kind enough, or loving enough, so you pretend to be more than you are. Maybe you're afraid of hurting someone's feelings so you wear a nice mask. Or you're insecure about your job so you wear a sincere and dependable mask. A gregarious mask is good to deflect real contact, avoid intimacy, or hide insecurity. There are thousands of masks.

Masks are repression, which is fear. There is no way to successfully repress who you are. It's like holding a rubber life raft under water. As long as you're willing to exert the effort you can do it, but eventually you're going to get tired and it will surface. A man represses his anger with his wife, but takes it out on his employees. A woman wears a fake smile all day at work; her repression takes the form of an ulcer. For years a man checks his emotional desires and the repression manifests as cancer. Repressed feelings will always come out.

Action required: 1. Understand why you wear the mask. What is the fear behind it? 2. Decide if the reason you wear it is valid anymore. Often it isn't. 3. Analyze the cost of wearing your mask. How is repression manifesting in your life? 4. Realize that all you have to do to remove your mask is be direct and honest in your communications with others.

Erica: Seminar Dialogue

"But if I were to be direct and honest with some of the people in my life they would hate me," said Erica. She was a woman in her early fifties. Her clothing would have been appropriate for an executive office.

"What you are saying, Erica, is they would hate you unless they can manipulate you to be what they want you to be instead of what you are. Do you need people like that in your life?"

"Oh-h-h-h! I see what you mean. Okay, let me ask you something else. I always have to act like I'm in control. It's almost more important than anything else in my life. Is that a mask?"

"Are you always in control?"

"Of course not, but I'm not about to let anyone else know that," she replied, straightening her shoulders and clearing her throat.

"The real you is sensitive, vulnerable, and is not always sure about the best way to handle things?" I asked lightly.

Her response was an amused nod.

"Then what is the cost of repressing who you really are?"

"The cost? Hm-m-m-m . . . I probably scare a lot of people off. Men I'd really like to know and get close to. And I have to spend a lot of alone time to recharge myself enough to go back out there and play the role of . . ."

"Superwoman?" I interrupted. She chuckled. "Let's look for the cause, Erica." She agreed and was quickly in deep hypnosis. I directed her back to the events responsible for her current need to appear in control.

"I'm in woods . . . dense woods and shells are exploding all around us. There's a cannon . . . old-fashioned type of . . . I'm so confused. So confused. I just don't know what to do." Her voice is deep and strained.

"Are you in command?"

"I am now. The captain's dead."

"All right . . . let's move forward a little ways into the future so you can tell me what happens. One, two, three."

"It was terrible. I let the men attempt to save themselves. We lost the position and the Germans broke through. Most of our men died. I could have saved many of them by grouping at the hilltop . . . and we would have held."

From her Higher Self perspective, I asked Erica to share her understanding. "I wasn't trained in that life to take command. I did the best I knew how, but it wasn't very effective. Now, I must separate the past from the present. No one will die today if I am not in control of the situation. My subconscious is shielding me from reexperiencing the guilt and pain of a time I didn't take control."

6. INCOMPATIBLE GOALS AND VALUES

If your goals and values are not compatible you will subconsciously block yourself from achieving your goals, or you'll change your values to make them consistent with your goals, or you'll destroy one or the other in the process. As an example, if your wife and family are your highest value, and your goal is to become a manufacturer's representative covering a five-state territory, your value and goal are inconsistent. Your work would necessitate travel, allowing minimal home life.

Action required: Recognize the incompatible goals and values. List your goals, one to ten, with the most important at the top, etc. Do the same with your values. Any great separation on the list will indicate that you need to rethink one or the other, to resolve or avoid a conflict.

Justin: Seminar Dialogue

"When I listed my life area values in the last group process, they were: 1. spirituality, 2. friends/associates, 3. community development, 4. education/intellectual development, 5. physical fitness/well-being, 6. recreation/leisure activities." Justin explained, looking up at me in confusion.

"So?" I said. "You're not very materialistic are you?"

"So, the following didn't even make my list—finances, career, emotions/love/sex, family life, physical environment, or material possessions. But on my list of goals, the top one is a million dollars."

I laughed out loud. "Who's fooling who, Justin?"

"I've been saying 'I want a million' to myself and everyone else for five years," he said seriously.

"Then it's time to stop fooling yourself, isn't it? If you want to make a million dollars, you've got to enjoy the game you play to attain the money, and you'd better have an emotional purpose behind the goal."

"What do you mean an emotional purpose?"

"Oh, fame, or glory, or to rebuild the family fortune, or send your children to Harvard, or to impress the woman that you want to marry. Something like that," I said. "Which are you willing to rethink, your goals or values?"

"Not my values," Justin quickly replied. His eyes grew openly amused, he smiled and sat down. "I don't know what I'd do with a million dollars if I had it," I heard him say quietly to the person sitting beside him.

7. RESISTANCE TO "WHAT IS"

It is your resistance to what is that causes your suffering. Freedom lies in the acceptance of what is, for when you recognize and accept things as they are, you stop wasting mental or physical energy attempting to change what cannot be changed. This is simple logic. There are things you have a potential to change, so go ahead and change them. Do everything you can to bring about the change. But there are also things you cannot change, so recognize these areas of your life and stop wasting your efforts. Most importantly, stop generating negative subconscious programming with your frustrations.

A Christian prayer says the same thing: "God grant me the serenity to accept the things I cannot change, the courage to change the things I can, and the wisdom to know the difference."

Action required: Accept the facts, logic, and unalterable realities in your life. Actually, you have no choice in accepting what is, but you have a choice in how you respond to what is.

Arlene: Seminar Dialogue
Arlene, an attractive woman in her mid-forties, raised her hand to share. When she received the microphone, she said, "For twenty-five years I've been at-

tempting to change my husband. He's so quiet it's almost impossible to get him to talk and when he does he's sarcastic.

"Every night after work, he stops for a drink at the bar with his friends. He constantly has me upset. Now, it sounds like you're saying to accept him just the way he is."

"*He* has upset you by being what he is?"

"He certainly has," she responded in a grudging voice. "If he was nicer and came home right after work, I'd be happier. If you think I'm going to stop trying to change him, you're crazy."

"Nothing has happened in twenty-five years. How long do you think it's going to take?" I asked, unable to suppress a smile.

"I just don't know."

"Arlene, how many hours of your marriage have you spent being upset over the way your husband is?"

"I don't know. Thousands and thousands, I suppose. Once I threatened to leave him unless he quit stopping at the bar. He did for two weeks, but he made my life so miserable it wasn't worth it." She sighed and slumped a little in a sympathy-seeking gesture.

"Arlene, your husband has never made you miserable. You've made yourself needlessly miserable for twenty-five years by resisting what he is. Plus, you've generated a lot of negative subconscious programming which has manifested as additional disharmony in your life."

"So you think I should give up after all this time?" she said, disbelief in her voice.

"Well, it seems to me you have three choices, Arlene. You can leave him. You can keep resisting him and be miserable. Or, if you're going to stay with him, accept him for what he is and spend your emotional energy constructively for a change. Your life will get better immediately because the negative self-programming will stop. If you change, he might even respond differently to the new, nicer you. Don't be blind to the logic."

"But that would be admitting I've wasted twenty-five years."

"You have Arlene. Your husband was perfect all along, and you didn't know it."

"PERFECT?" Her voice was sarcastic and her brows furrowed in an angry frown.

"Well, since you now realize you can't change him, doesn't it make sense to accept him as he is? That's basic, simple logic. And if you accept him as he is, he's perfect from your perspective. You can't accept him and not accept him at the same time. Besides, unless you accept him, you'll have to come back together in similar circumstances in a future life."

Arlene's frown deepened, but she didn't respond, so I continued. "Your husband is your karma. He's here to teach you to accept what is. Isn't that nice?" I flashed a large, friendly smile.

"You're as bad as he is," she said, sitting down.

8. MIRRORING

The positive or negative qualities you react to in others are a reflection of the same qualities within you. Other people are a mirror for you, and if you are aware, you will learn from the mirror. If you see fear in someone else, you're recognizing fear within yourself. If you think someone is selfish and it bothers you, be aware there is selfishness within you. Anything in another person that really bothers you, or attracts you, exists in you.

Action required: Examine your reactions to others by searching yourself for the corresponding trait. If your reaction is negative, it is rooted in a fear—which you are here on earth to resolve. Learn to see people you dislike as mirrors instead of adversaries.

Spencer: Seminar Dialogue

"I'm having a hard time with that concept, Richard," Spencer said. His arms were crossed tightly across his chest, one hand raised just enough to hold the microphone. "I'm really bothered by the irrational actions of some of the world's leaders. They certainly aren't a mirror for me."

"You're never irrational?" I asked.

"Well . . . yes, but not on that scale. Their actions affect millions," he said.

"Scale has nothing to do with it. When were you most irrational?"

He hesitated, then replied. "During my divorce, I suppose. Okay, got it. But what about an attention seeker? There is a flamboyant woman in our office who literally drives me crazy. She has to have attention, and if she can't get it one way, she'll find another. She wears wild clothes, crazy hats, and brings in beautifully decorated birthday cakes for staffers. If you don't go out of your way to acknowledge her, she does something to attract your attention. Now I don't see myself in her— I'm quiet and go out of my way to avoid attracting attention."

"No way, Spencer. If you're that bothered by her, you really need to attract attention in some area of your life," I said. "What do you do for a living?"

"I'm an advertising agency art director."

"Interesting. I'm very familiar with art directors. And I've yet to meet a good one that didn't enter his best work in the annual art shows, hoping to take some awards. Awards are great ego boosters, they enhance your reputation in the field and get you a higher salary when you move on to your next job. It's a more subtle way of getting attention, but . . ." I stood looking at Spencer, without saying anything.

"Well, sure. I want respect within the agency and in my field."

"You'd really like to be thought of as one of the top art directors in Los Angeles, wouldn't you?"

"Of course."

"Why does this bother you?"

"It doesn't."

"Yes it does, Spencer, or you wouldn't be bothered by the attention seeker in your office."

He took a deep breath and expelled it with a gusty sigh. Keeping his arms crossed on his chest, he looked at the floor, then frowned at me. "Well, the ad field is obsessed with who's hot, and what concepts are hot, and who can steal whose account, and who takes the most awards in this year's show. It gets old. Once you have a reputation, it's a never-ending battle to retain it."

"So you let your creative work attract attention and enhance your reputation. In her way, the woman in your office uses wild clothes and birthday cakes to do the same thing. She's a mirror for your fear of maintaining your reputation."

Spencer silently mouthed a four-letter word as he sat down.

9. FEAR

Fear is a big word. All disturbances between human beings, large or small, interpersonal or international, are rooted in fear. Fear means all the negative emotions such as anger, selfishness, jealousy, hate, repression, envy, possessiveness, greed, anxiety, guilt, insecurity, inhibitions, vanity, malice, resentment,

blame, etc. The fears work against your spiritual evolution, and they can paralyze you—keeping you from
acting when you need to act. They can stop you from
making a growth choice when it would be in your best
interest.

Action required: Discover the cause of the fear if
possible. Often it is of value to confront your fear by
gathering the courage to act anyway. By totally experiencing the fear you will often rise above the effects of
the fear in your life.

Marilyn: Seminar Dialogue

"I'm very possessive of my husband and I understand that it's a fear of losing him. But he has never
done anything to make me feel insecure in any way,"
Marilyn said. She was attractive, in her early thirties,
and dressed in white cotton beach attire.

"Are you possessive about other people in your
life?" I asked. "Are you possessive of material possessions?"

"No, not of people or things," she replied. "That's
why it just doesn't make any sense. But it's there. And
I'm not just a little possessive. I'm *really* possessive."

Marilyn agreed to use regressive hypnosis to go
back to the cause. After directing her through time I
asked her to relate her understanding to me.

"I'm on a dock. The harbor is filled with old
sailing ships and there are people dressed in funny
clothes. Oh. I'm saying good-bye to someone. Ah . . . I
think he's my fiancé. Yes, he is dressed as a sailor and
he's kissing me good-bye."

"How long will he be gone?"

"I don't know. A long time. But we're going to get
married when he comes home."

"All right, move forward in time until something important happens in regard to your relationship."

"I don't believe it. I don't believe it." Her voice was pained. "I waited over a year for him, counting the days. And now his mates tell me he jumped ship and married a woman in England." Tears began running down her cheeks.

After directing her into her Higher Self, I asked her to explain her possessiveness.

"Obviously, I am afraid since he left me once, he will do it again. But I need to realize that my fear could create a problem where none exists. The tighter I attempt to hold onto him, the more he will want to be free. I'm also getting that it would be a karmic mistake to do something to even the score in this lifetime."

10. THE NEED TO BE RIGHT

Your subconscious mind is a memory bank and operates very much like a computer. It's programmed for survival and for you to be "right." Everything you consider saying or doing is quickly run through your data banks, comparing the present to related past experiences. Your computer then approves your actions as compared to the past, for in the past you survived.

Computers are logically programmed machines and cannot be wrong. To be wrong is a malfunction. If your subconscious computer allowed you to be wrong, survival is threatened. So, the only way it can work is to make you feel correct. It doesn't reason and it doesn't care if you get what you want out of life. It just needs to be correct to protect itself, even if you lose the game.

Action required: Learn to be aware of your programming so you begin to detach from the buttons that cause you to act like a robot. A robot has no choice in the way it acts. It has wiring and circuits that are set so when a button is pushed, it reacts according to programming. In many areas of your life you are programmed the same way. When your button is pushed you need to be right. Even if you're not right, you'll find some way to twist it around to justify yourself. Only those with enlightened awareness of how human beings work understand this. Winning the game is far more satisfying than getting to be right.

Anita: Seminar Dialogue

"Can the need to be right come from past-life programming?" asked Anita, a pretty woman in her mid-twenties.

"We're all programmed to need to be right, just as we are programmed to stand and walk on our feet," I replied. "But an excessive need to be right might go back to an event in past lives."

"But what do you do? My fiancé has to be right about everything, all the time. No one else is ever right. It's enough to drive you nuts." She rolled her eyes at the ceiling and drew her lips in thoughtfully.

"Do you want to remain with him?"

"Of course. I love him."

"Then you'd better develop an enlightened attitude allowing him to be right while you win the game. You have to learn to override your own 'rightness' button. Knowing how he is programmed to function, you can let him be right. Remember, unless you allow him to be right, his survival is threatened and there is going to be trouble. So you can quickly allow him to be right with a phrase such as, 'Yes, John, I understand that.' You're not admitting he is right, you're just taking him off tilt. His survival will no longer be threatened and he can concentrate upon the problem."

11. EXPECTATIONS

Expectations of a forthcoming experience will seldom serve you, for if the experience doesn't live up to your expectations, you'll be disappointed or unable to enjoy it for what it is.

Expectations of other people will never serve you. Whenever you expect someone else to be the way you want them to be, you're likely to be dissatisfied. No one can change someone else, nor can they expect another person to be anything other than what they are. When you insist that someone act according to your rules, they are forced to repress what they really are. Since long-term repression is impossible, the forced change will not last or it will result in new eruptions of unsatisfactory behavior.

Action required: Attain a self-actualized perspective of the futility of expectations of others. Since it is impossible to change people, accept them as they are without resisting what is.

Kent: Seminar Dialogue

"That's ridiculous. I just had lunch at a restaurant and the waitress was surly, and she brought me cold food. Since I'm paying for it, I certainly have a right to expect nice service and warm food," Kent said with authority. He was in his late thirties and dressed in casual, trendy attire.

"But obviously your expectations were in conflict with what is. What did you do?" I asked.

"I got very angry. It turned into a terrible scene."

"And how do you feel about it right now?"

"I'm still upset."

"So, you've sent a lot of negative programming to

your subconscious mind. What good did it do you, Kent?"

"What do you mean?"

"I mean what good did it do you? You got to be right, you caused a scene, and if you ate at all, you ate cold food. After the scene you probably felt uncomfortable. Maybe you got indigestion. What good did it do?"

"I hope I got the waitress fired."

"A lot of good that did you. Maybe you got to 'be right,' but you didn't win the game. Now in addition to negative programming, no lunch, embarrassment, and indigestion, now you've created a karmic enemy who will want to get even in your next life. Besides, that waitress usually isn't surly. It's just that she broke up with her boyfriend last night and she's very depressed about it."

"Jeez-z-z-z," Kent exclaimed in frustration. "So what do you advocate, just taking it from everybody?"

"I advocate that you be assertive and stand up for your human rights. But you made the whole situation worse for yourself. That's self-destructive. I'm sure five different enlightened people would have handled the situation five different ways, but they would have avoided being self-destructive."

"Give me an example?" Kent asked. His tone was coolly disapproving.

"You might have called the manager, calmly registered your complaints, refused to pay for lunch, then left."

"But I put up with rude service and received cold food."

"Right. And that's *what is*. Nothing was going to change that reality. You had two choices: 1. resisting what is and making it worse for yourself, or 2. accepting what is and handling the situation with minimal personal inconvenience."

"I see," he said slowly. "You always have a choice of making it better or worse. But if you feel anger you shouldn't suppress it."

"I agree. But wisdom will eventually override your automatic anger response. Once you truly accept an enlightened perspective you won't choose anger because it won't serve you."

Kent nodded. The corners of his lips turned up in a slight smile. "Thanks," he said.

12. CLARITY OF INTENT

The primary reason people are not as happy or successful as they desire to be is they are not clear on their intent. In other words, they don't know exactly what they want. If you don't know what you want, how do you expect to get it? In the seminars—even when people appear to be clear about what they want in life—when I process them, their confusion becomes obvious. All too often their wants are based upon what they think they *should* want, or what they think their friends or family want. Maybe they feel their real wants are greedy, so they disguise them. Others feel their real wants are irresponsible or unrealistic, so they won't admit to them.

Action required: 1. To unleash the unlimited power of your mind, you have to be honest with yourself about what you want. 2. Discover what is blocking you from getting it. It will be one of three things: A. A subconscious fear; B. A negative payoff; C. It is a totally unrealistic goal. 3. Decide what you are willing to pay to get what you want. The price will be one or more of the following: A. Money; B. Effort; C. Sacrifice.

Once you have this awareness, you will decide to accomplish your goal or you will accept that it isn't what you want. Either way, your life will work better for you will no longer be dealing with illusion.

Carol: Seminar Dialogue

"What if you just don't know what you want?" asked Carol. She was fortyish with short hair and an infectious grin. She was dressed in a bulky sweater and jeans.

"Well, what if, like Dorothy in *The Wizard of Oz,* you could click your heels together and have anything you wanted?" I asked.

"Anything?"

I nodded in reply. She thought for a long moment before answering. "I've always wanted to be a singer, but it's a little late for that."

"Not necessarily," I replied. "Can you sing?"

"Yes, I have a very good voice."

"Then how could you incorporate singing into your life-style?"

"It would be impossible. I have to support myself and I couldn't travel."

"Argue for your limitations and they shall be yours. I think Richard Bach wrote that," I said. "Never assume there is only one way to fulfill your desires. I know a lot of singers. My father-in-law sings in local opera productions. He works a regular job, but his after-work activities center around the opera group. That's where he finds his joy. Another friend of mine sings jingles and creates music for commercials. She started out part-time while holding down another job, but as the demand for her services grew, so did her income. Now music is her full-time occupation. I'm sure there are hundreds of other approaches."

"I see," she said thoughtfully. "But do you really think you can do anything you want?"

"As long as your goal doesn't manipulate another human being, and if you're willing to pay the price. Every 'I want' has a price tag. And your goal must be realistic. If you're sixty years old and have no background in politics, I doubt that you can be President of the United States. If you're tone deaf, a career as a singer isn't realistic."

"I don't know that you're serving people by telling them things like this," she said. Her voice was resigned. "It could cause people to dream foolish dreams."

"Is there such a thing as a foolish dream?" I asked.

13. LACK OF ALIVENESS OR MOTIVATION

Aliveness is real enjoyment in doing what you do. It's excitement . . . exhilaration that makes you feel glad to be alive. It's the joy, stimulation, and pleasure that makes life worth living. The best way I've found to generate aliveness and motivation is to get someone to do what they really want to do. What you want to do is always your best option in life, because life appears to be set up for you to get what you want—*if* you dare to want it. So, when you are making choices, do what you want most—*not* which choice makes the most sense.

Action required: To overcome lack of aliveness and motivate yourself, get involved in what really interests you. It is important to realize that you must have strength-producing activity in your life or you will become depressed. Your mind will never allow your life to become too boring and mundane without doing something to make it more interesting. The problem is, it might generate fights with your mate (when you hurt, at least you know you're alive), or an illness (kidney stones would give you something to talk about), or an accident (endangering your life will create a lot of aliveness). The idea is to make life interesting before your mind does it for you.

Marina: Seminar Dialogue

"I understand what you just said about Dorothy in *The Wizard of Oz,* but that doesn't resolve it for me. Maybe I'm a dummy, but I still don't really know what I want out of life," Marina said, as she raised her hands in a gesture of futility. She was dressed in a designer jumpsuit and wore a wistful expression on her face.

"You're not a dummy, Marina, and you're not alone. How many people in this room are willing to admit that they really don't know exactly what they want out of life? Be straight!" I raised my hand, indicating I wanted them to raise theirs if they were not clear on their intent. Half the hands in a ballroom of three hundred people were raised.

Marina looked around. She shrugged her shoulders and said, "Guess I'm not alone, but that doesn't make me feel any better."

"All right, Marina, I would suggest that you and everyone who just raised their hand put first things first. Make it a priority to discover what would generate happiness and fulfillment for you. Happiness and fulfillment comes from within, not from another person. Someone else can add to your happiness but they can't make you happy. It's time to dream your dreams. It's time to ask yourself, What do I really enjoy doing? What do I do naturally and well?

"Enjoyment comes from the God portion of your totality," I continued. "If you want to express your Godliness, do only what you enjoy in life. If you don't enjoy it, don't do it. Delegate it to someone who enjoys it. You might have to work a little longer at what you enjoy to earn the money to hire someone to do what you don't enjoy. But that's fine, do it. Some of you are saying to yourself, 'how silly, how stupid.' You're arguing for your limitations and reducing your options. And if you do that in this training room with me, you do it in the rest of your life.

"We're here on earth to learn to let go of fear and to learn to express unconditional love. As part of the process we learn that life is what we make it. And hopefully we learn the most important lesson of all." I slowly scanned the room, making eye contact with as many people as possible. "LIFE IS TO BE EN-JOYED!"

About the Author

DICK SUTPHEN (pronounced Sut-fen) is an author, past-life therapist and seminar trainer. His best-selling books, *You Were Born Again to Be Together; Past Lives, Future Loves;* and *Unseen Influences,* have become classic metaphysical titles (Pocket Books).

Sutphen is the author of 10 metaphysical books and over 300 self-help tapes, including past-life regression programs. He has a twenty-year background in New Age work and research. Today, he conducts his world-famous seminar trainings throughout the country. Since 1977, 75,000 people have attended. Dick also publishes *Master of Life,* a free, quarterly publication that promotes mental, physical and philosophical self-sufficiency, and keeps readers abreast of his latest research and findings.

Dick and his wife, Tara, live in Malibu, California, where he writes and directs his New Age communications network. To receive a copy of *Master of Life* magazine, please write: Dick Sutphen, Box 38, Malibu, CA 90265.